Dear WONDERFUL *You,*

LETTERS TO ADOPTED & FOSTERED YOUTH

EDITORS:
DIANE RENÉ CHRISTIAN
& MEI-MEI AKWAI ELLERMAN, PHD

Dear Wonderful You, Letters to Adopted & Fostered Youth

Edited and Compiled By: Mei-Mei Akwai Ellerman PhD & Diane René Christian

First Print Edition: 2014

ISBN-13: 978-1502746658
ISBN-10: 1502746654

Cover and Formatting: Streetlight Graphics

THE ᴀɴ-ʏᴀ Pʀᴏᴊᴇᴄᴛ

An-Ya and Her Diary: The Novel (April, 2012)
An-Ya and Her Diary: Reader & Parent Guide (April, 2013)
Perpetual Child: Adult Adoptee Anthology (November, 2013)
Dear Wonderful You, Letters to Adopted & Fostered Youth (2014)

For more information on the AN-YA Project visit:
www.anyadiary.com

M<small>Y PEN IS FINALLY TOUCHING</small> your pages. It is time to tell our story. Our story began in China and now it continues in America. I want to write about our old life and I want to write about our life now. I will write it all down with hopes that somehow I can connect the two worlds that I have lived in. Right now those worlds seem so far apart. I don't know if it is possible for my world to ever feel whole, without a crack down the middle...but it is time to try.

An-Ya
安雅

From the novel *An-Ya and Her Diary*
(2012 by Diane René Christian)

Table Of Contents

LETTERS TO ADOPTED & FOSTERED YOUTH

Dedication

THE GIFT OF LETTER WRITING

THE LETTERS NESTLED BETWEEN THE covers of this anthology are our collective gift. Each one is a small work of art, written painstakingly and with great heart. We, the authors, have reached deep within ourselves and overcome personal challenges to share our thoughts, feelings, even painful memories from our past. Individually composed for your eyes only, this collection arose from the wish to convey our private messages in everlasting book form. We hope that you will treasure "Dear Wonderful You," carefully safeguard it, and in time, when you feel ready, share it with family and friends. May the letters in this volume be handled with reverence and love, and then, even if yellowed, brittle and crumbling, passed on to the next generation and many others thereafter, in remembrance and in honor of our common struggles and triumphs.

As your older fostered and or adopted sisters and brothers, we have navigated through the turbulent waters of childhood and adolescence and have now moved into our more mature years, paving the way for you. We hope that our stories will bring you solace, laughter, inspiration and yes, even tears. Each letter was written expressly for you, to be read in the privacy of your room, under the shade of a willow tree, strolling through a meadow of billowing grasses or a symphony of wild flowers. Please cherish our gift and hold it close to your heart. We trust that some accounts may reflect your own experiences and others will inspire you. May this book give you the courage to set out on your ongoing journey, knowing that you are embraced, supported at every step and that you belong to a loving family of older siblings who will always stand by you.

-Mei-Mei Akwai Ellerman, PhD

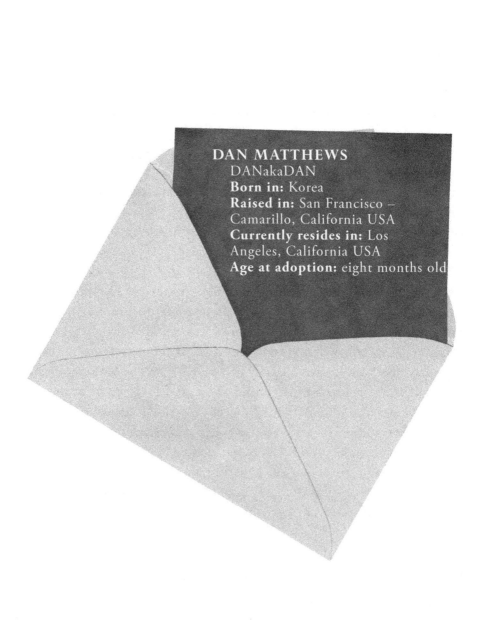

DAN MATTHEWS
DANakaDAN
Born in: Korea
Raised in: San Francisco –
Camarillo, California USA
Currently resides in: Los
Angeles, California USA
Age at adoption: eight months old

Is There Anybody Out There?

Is there anybody, anyone who's watching over,
I believe in god, but I question as I get older
Will my burdens he shoulder, can I remain a soldier
Between doing what is right sometimes, and what I know is colder
And it's a scary proposition from this place of my vision
When I can't even trust myself with simple moral decisions
I know it's wrong for me to question or even trying to test you
But it's hard sometimes when I stare at myself in the restroom
That's why can I be open, can I say I took it for granted
Of what could be offered in life, this is my time to be candid
Never mind, I'll just get faded, besides thinking is overrated
And I just want to escape, than to face what I've created
So tell me is there anybody out, that you know without a doubt
Can explain to me all this, and what life is all about

Chorus:
Is there anybody out there?
Hope they're still waiting for me
Cuz I'm feeling so scared
But I know through this I can be free
Cuz if I keep on I know I'll find
It'll all get better in time
Is anybody out there?
Cuz I know they're still waiting,
You're still waiting on me

—

Lyrics by Dan Matthews
DANakaDAN

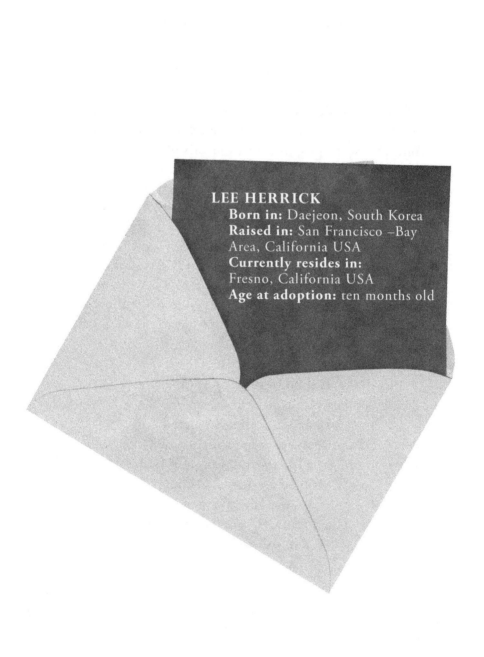

LEE HERRICK
  Born in: Daejeon, South Korea
  Raised in: San Francisco –Bay
  Area, California USA
  Currently resides in:
  Fresno, California USA
  Age at adoption: ten months old

Salvation

The blues is what mothers do not tell their sons,
in church or otherwise, how their bodies forgave
them when their spirits gave in, how you salvage love
by praying for something acoustic, something clean

and simple like the ideal room, one with a shelf
with your three favorite books and a photo
from your childhood, the one of you with the
big grin before you knew about the blues.

I wonder what songs my birth mother sang in
the five months she fed me before she left me
on the steps of a church in South Korea.
I wonder if they sounded like Sarah Chang's

quivering bow, that deep chant of a mother
saying goodbye to her son. Who can really say?
Sometimes all we have is the blues. The blues means
finding a song in the abandonment, one

you can sing in the middle of the night when
you remember that your Korean name, Kwang Soo
Lee, means bright light, something that can illuminate
or shine, like tears, little drops of liquefied God,

glistening down your brown face. I wonder
what songs my birth mother sings and if she sings
them for me, what stories her body might tell.
I have come to believe that the blues is the body's

salvation, a chorus of scars to remind you
that you are here, not where you feared you would be,
but here, flawed, angelic, and full of light.
I believe that the blues is the spirit's wreckage,

examined and damaged but whole again, more full
and prepared than it's ever been, quiet and still,
just as it was always meant to be.

Message of Support from Lee Herrick

OUR VOICES MATTER. YOUR VOICE matters. Over the years, my voice has been shaped by a number of people and experiences, and as an author, it continues to evolve. I often hear from readers whose lives have been touched by my work. This was the case recently, when a high school teacher told me that a student of hers discovered my poem, "Salvation," in a time of need. The student was struggling with her identity. Teachers, counselors, and therapists worked with her. Her voice was forming, but she was suffering from depression. According to her teacher, the student read my poem for an assignment in class and was immediately moved by it. There was something in it that resonated with her. The student photocopied it, drew small flowers and hearts in its margins, and taped it to the front of her three-ring binder. Her depression began to show signs of improvement. Her teacher wrote me a long letter, explaining how my poem helped the student. To say I was touched would be a great understatement. It is deeply gratifying to know that this played a role in Co-editor Diane René Christian's decision to create a book of letters to adopted and fostered youth. Your voices are beautiful. If the story of your youth contains gaps, it does not mean you are not whole. I hope the letters in this book provide you moments of light, insight, and inspiration. Whether it takes the form of a poem, a song, a story, or a dance, I hope you find, develop, and share your voice. It is beautiful and important. To the high school student who read my poem and to every other beautiful adoptee and fostered youth of any age and any background, I wish you happiness, health, and peace.

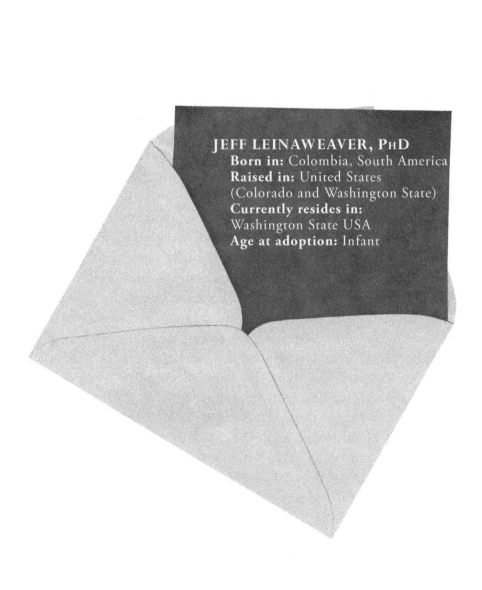

JEFF LEINAWEAVER, PhD
  Born in: Colombia, South America
  Raised in: United States
  (Colorado and Washington State)
  Currently resides in:
  Washington State USA
  Age at adoption: Infant

Dear Wonderful You,

I'VE ALWAYS TOLD MY DAUGHTERS there's a unique story trying to live through you. This is a gift, and includes our storylines of being orphaned and adopted. I say "our" storylines because I was also orphaned and adopted just like my daughters; my father, too!

You see, I come from a family with three generations of adoption, two of which are from Colombia. We are very proud about the uniqueness of our family roots. It's just been our fate and destiny story.

Now, despite saying all this, and feeling quite comfortable about being adopted, I never quite know how to start a conversation about international adoption, or about being an "international adoptee" or my own personal view on international adoption.

This is sometimes awkward, in part, because I have spent the majority of my life living outside international adoptee culture. In fact, I did not meet another person internationally adopted until the age of 37. While this may seem crazy, neither my father nor I identified with the label of being an "international adoptee."

Instead, we have always just seen ourselves as people who just happened to be adopted by way of the interesting synchronicities of fate and destiny, also known to us as being orphaned and adopted.

The gift of growing up outside international adoptee culture, or essentially "off the grid" has given me an appreciation for my own story, a confidence, as well as having fresh eyes on the experience of adoption. This is a lived experience with many truths and viewpoints. This is a good thing, I think. What's yours?

One story we as a family have told is one that sees all human beings, whether adopted or not, as children of fate and destiny. This is a universal idea that has really made me feel more equal, coming from the same place of mystery that everyone else does, too. It has

19

helped me erase and heal from stories others have had about me, telling me I don't belong, or how my family isn't my "real family," or I'm separate, or alone. Through this perspective of personal mythology, and my fate and destiny story, it has helped me feel rooted in the right place, with the right people, and just know that, I am where I am where I am, good or bad, it just is. The fate of my family's stories has been my kin as much as they have been handed down to me to soothe myself and live within. It's allowed me to learn how to practice the making of my destiny through the stories lived, stories told and the stories I continue to tell.

Throughout human history, particularly in storytelling, drama and mythology, orphans and adoptees have been defined by fate and destiny stories.

Which stories do you know that have heroes who are adopted? Now, my father was a professor of theatre and I'm a storyteller, so we are certainly more "open" to the ideas of fate and destiny and the importance of story and dreams. That said, this perspective has also been the key to understanding our own heroic journeys. Some of the greatest heroes have been orphans and adoptees. Why not us?

Now, I recognize this is a pretty different point of view, but it's one that has also empowered me to embrace the ownership of my own adoption story. This has helped me realize that to live our own unique story, we must learn how to become our own heroes. To be our own heroes, I've learned that we must also learn how to heal our own wounds in our own ways sometimes, even if that doesn't make any sense to others, particularly those not-adopted. It's ok. I believe.

As children of fate and destiny, I see each birth story as one that includes hints of an inner myth trying to enter the world through us. As human beings, we are mythic by nature, each carrying the thread of a unique plotline that seeks to unfold throughout the course of life.

This point of view has also taught me that we must also learn to be careful to whom we tell our stories sometimes, and that it's not ok for others to tell our stories for us, or in our name for our benefit, or theirs. In the culture of international adoption, many people like to tell your story for you, put words in your mouth, or want to be your hero for you.

Most importantly, through the deepening of my own understanding of my family's mythic origin narrative, and in embracing others as being children of fate and destiny, too, I have experienced the creativity, serendipity and mystery of what Joseph Campbell called "a thousand unseen helping hands." I've never felt, "alone," and so I hope you know that you aren't alone.

We deserve to own our own story and heroic journey. Believe in yourself and your story. More importantly, understand that the point of being a hero is to do and be something greater than oneself, to give back to others. Keep this in the back of your mind as you grow and live your life. Don't allow being adopted, or orphaned get in the way of your heroic story, allow it to guide your own unique voice in the world, to be a new story, your story. That's why you are you!

I believe we, those internationally adopted, have heroic work to do in the world, to make it a better place, to help heal. Our stories matter, they are the gift to the world, and this includes the good and the bad. I encourage you to nurture and protect your own stories, and celebrate you as the hero you've been waiting for.

Kindest Regards,
Jeff

ROSITA GONZALEZ
Born: Somewhere near Seoul, Korea
Raised in: Georgia, Kansas, Oklahoma and finally Tennessee USA
Currently resides in: Midwest, USA
Age at adoption: 13 months
Age fostered: 6 months to 12 months

Dear Wonderful You,

I AM MUCH LIKE YOU, THOUGH I am 46 years old. "How's that?" you might ask.

Well, two years ago, I met my first Korean adult adoptee. Just imagine. I lived 44 years never knowing another Korean adoptee.

When I was your age (Don't you just hate it when grownups say that?) ... okay, how about this ... in the 1980s, I was a teenager in a small, Tennessee town. I was one of two Asians in my school; the other was a Thai boy my age. We were often paired for square dances by the teachers and coupled by our fellow classmates.

I, of course, rebelled. I was not THAT kind of Asian with the smelly food and poor fashion sense. I was a judgmental teen in a small town, but I couldn't hide my race, nor that I was adopted. I would go home and look over the adoption agency's monthly magazine, filled with portraits of adoptees. I wished I could mingle with them; they would understand what it meant to be the Asian in a sea of white.

But in East Tennessee, there was no such community. I felt lonely, misunderstood and isolated. Teasing about my race became commonplace, but I didn't want to trouble my parents. They loved me and would feel the pain I felt. I feared hurting them as I had been hurt. So, I was silent.

I hope that you don't feel that pain, and if you do, that you will share it with someone. I would gladly lend an ear.

Today, I am finally happy in my skin because I found my village. I found a home with a group of adult adoptees. Some are transracial adoptees and international adoptees like me, and some are domestic American adoptees.

We share common threads ... our experiences, our struggles, our pasts. It feels good to talk to people who have the same struggles. I encourage you to do the same. I know that sometimes, the culture camps and other adoptee gatherings might seem like a drag. I know you just want to be thought of as "normal" like everyone else. I know you don't want your adoption to define you as a person. I have been there. I have pushed well-meaning Asians away from me. That hanging thread always emerges. Either you snip it or you weave it back in. Even if you snip it, a piece remains, and one day, it will wiggle its way back out.

As a grownup, I eventually decided I needed to address this loose thread. Some brilliant Asian sisters, while not adopted, have taught me so much about my Asian culture. They have embraced my children and taught us about Korean customs and foods. Now, I relish my relationships with these Asian women; they are my best friends.

With the technology you have these days, you can be in contact with many more adoptees than I ever imagined. These adoptees will be your village when you grow older, and opportunities to meet new people dwindle. Yeah, we grownups have a hard time finding our communities. "Old and set in our ways," as my mother once said. (And insert here my teen eye-roll.) But we are.

Cherish those adoptee friendships now; they will help you down the road.

And if you need it, I'm listening.

Sincerely,
Rosita
(The 46YO you.)

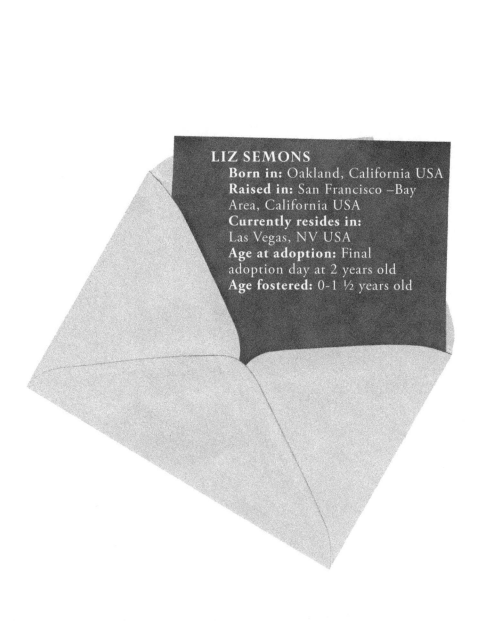

LIZ SEMONS
Born in: Oakland, California USA
Raised in: San Francisco –Bay Area, California USA
Currently resides in: Las Vegas, NV USA
Age at adoption: Final adoption day at 2 years old
Age fostered: 0-1 ½ years old

Dear Wonderful You,

I AM NOT SURE WHAT YOUR name is, but I already know one thing about you. That you are WONDERFUL! It is because I know this that I cannot wait to know your name. Why? Because you are "like me" and I am pretty cool if I do say so myself! I bet you are just as cool and have a good heart, spirit, and smile. I have met quite a few other adoptees in my time and to be honest with you, they are my kind of people. I find them to be more "real" than others and they are great friends. So, I am just looking for some more good friends and I hope you are interested in being my friend. I still need others that "get it" to talk with and I bet you might as well. Being adopted is not really always an easy thing, is it?

Since you are "like me" I bet some days you probably feel happier than others. I bet there are days that you do not think much about being different and then maybe days where being different overwhelms you and is on your mind quite a bit. This is how it was for me. I would go through periods when all of the sudden I would think about—

I wonder who I really am?

I wonder who my mom is?

I wonder who my dad is?

I wonder if my sisters and brothers know about me?

I wonder if I have sisters and brothers?

I wonder if they look like me?

I bet we would have been best friends.

It is too bad that I do not know them, because I could really use a good friend right now.

I wonder if they know how alone I feel?

I wonder if they think about me?

27

I wonder if my mom knows it's my birthday?
I wonder why she gave me up?
I wonder why they adopted me?
I wonder why I get treated differently from their "real kids"?

The list goes on. There are many thoughts that we as adoptees have and they are normal since essentially we really do not know who we are as many of us do not know where we came from. That is what makes you so wonderful to me. You understand what I just said. Not everybody can do that. They do not "get it."

The fact that you may have these same thoughts and desires to know what most people around you take for granted makes you a special person to me. I just wanted you to know that!

When you have days where you feel lost, insecure or confused or just want to talk, know that you have an adopted friend named Liz. And I am here. (I really am) I am 45 years old born in 1968. Being bi-racial back then already made me different so being adopted on top of that had many challenges in me figuring out who I was. It can be really hard but it can also be done. I just strived to remain good and to remain strong and it is a good thing because being adopted requires a lot of strength. But the main thing to remember for people "like us" is that we are not alone. Back in my time I swear I thought I was alone and it was SCARY! I did not realize that there are millions of adoptees worldwide and many of us wonder *"Why Me?"*

I was adopted when I was one and a half years old. I first went to a foster home as I was given up at birth. I am black and Irish and I was adopted by a Caucasian family so I was reminded everyday how different I was as I did not look like anybody in my family. Life has had many ups and downs and twists and turns. Being adopted has always been a huge part of who I am and I think this is because it is all I knew. Even something as simple as going to the doctor and them asking, "What is your medical history?" is a reminder when you have to answer, "I don't know? I am adopted." So, being adopted never really goes away. This is why I find connecting to others "like us" so healing and rewarding. It really feels like a sense of family when you know you can talk to others that understand and feel the same pain that you may feel. It has not been easy, but it has helped me. I realize now that for me it is necessary to know that I am not alone even at

45 years of age. I know you are probably thinking, "She is old! I do not want to talk to her!" But I am a cool 45-year-old with a lot of kid in me! I like to write songs and rap too!

How about I don't tell you my whole life story but if I share some lyrics to a song/rap that I wrote that sums it all up? I sometimes express myself best this way. So this is my song called:

PAIN, PAIN CAN YOU GO AWAY?

Pain, Pain Can you go away? Cause this girl needs brighter days
People that see me once in a while
Don't know that they looking at a fake smile
Cause they really don't know what I've been through
They really don't care so I don't share
Adopted Dad Adopted Mom
But still out getting my hustle on
Cause they really didn't want me
But that's ok
Determined to make it anyway
Pain, Pain Can you go away? Cause this girl needs brighter days
I'm black and white
Trying to live my life right
I never really fit in anywhere
One day I said it don't matter and I don't care
You either like me or you don't
It's up to you, but this bad girl gonna do what she do
Pain, Pain can you go away Cause this girl needs brighter days
Lost and confused is how I feel
Cause it's so hard to find people that are real
When I put myself out there I always get played
But I still keep hope for better days
Pain, Pain can you go away? Cause this girl needs brighter days
Cold Cold world out here on your own
It's a do or die and I had to survive
So I took one day at a time
But I wondered what I did for this life of mine
Brighter Days, Brighter Days, Brighter Days I pray for:
Brighter Days!

Although my life has had many ups and downs— today I am strong, independent and happy. I hope my words and lyrics bring inspiration that brighter days can and will come.

Stay Wonderful! Stay You!
Your adopted friend,
Liz

KAREN PICKELL
Born in: Cleveland, OH USA
Raised in: Cleveland, OH USA
Currently resides in: Tampa
Bay area, FL USA
Age at adoption: 3 ½ months

Dear Wonderful You,

LOOK INTO THE MIRROR. WHAT do you see? I already know: You are beautiful.

You don't see it? Are you not beautiful? I know that you are. But I know, too, that you may not be able to see yourself as beautiful.

Beautiful. What does it mean?

We learn the words we know by hearing them from others. Maybe you have never heard this word, *beautiful,* directed toward you. Maybe it is only an idea from a song or a movie—a celebrity's face, a dress someone wore, a note written to a crush. It is not about you.

No one called me beautiful when I was growing up. I wondered, why are all the other daughters beautiful but I am not? Why am I the strange one, with orange hair and pale skin, with blisters rather than a tan in the summer and freckles covering my arms and face all year long? Why am I the one who can't wear pink because of my coloring but must always wear bangs because of my high forehead? Why are my eyelashes so light but my eyebrows so thick and dark?

No one I knew looked like me. Yes, there were redheads at school, but they had suitable names beginning with "Mc" or "Mac" and they knew the meanings of those Celtic words on the St. Patrick's Day slogans. They lived in houses full of siblings all fair and freckled as themselves, all fine-looking to each other.

I was beautiful to no one.

Then in ninth grade, a boy noticed me. He liked how I looked. He didn't call me beautiful, but he liked my gray eyes and the freckle on my top lip. He didn't call me pretty, but he liked the way I wore a t-shirt and how toned my legs looked during the summer when I rode my bike a lot. He wanted to look at me and to touch me. No one ever touched me at home—no hugs when I returned from school in the afternoons, no kisses before I went to bed at night. This boy kissed me all the time and hugged me, too. He liked to hug me tight.

But he never, ever said I was beautiful, not on any of the days we were together, not even during those weeks when he was grounded for his poor grades and claimed to miss me so very much.

When you never have a word thrown your direction, it's difficult to catch what it means.

When I was a young woman in my twenties and living on my own, I would not even run to the store to pick up something to eat without first spending an hour curling my hair and applying my makeup. I had learned from magazines how to make myself appear attractive. I memorized all the steps they listed to make hair seem thicker, eyes seem larger, skin seem smoother, smile seem brighter. I was an artist creating a girl no one could think less of, a girl who was just like all the other girls. They could all be seen without makeup, of course, while I would forever need a case full of beauty products to make myself acceptable.

I did not understand beauty. The longer I lived without it, the more beauty seemed to be just a model's face on a magazine cover, something I could paint on myself to make people love me. Because I did understand that everyone loved beautiful things. If I was not beautiful, then I was unlovable.

I wanted to be beautiful because I wanted to be loved.

Think about someone you love. Picture the shape of her eyes, the length of her nose. Imagine the color of his hand, the texture of his hair. He's beautiful, isn't he? Isn't she so very pretty?

Have you ever seen an ugly puppy? Or an unlovable kitten? Of course not. There is no such thing.

Nor is there such a thing as an ugly child. All children are beautiful. I was a beautiful child. I see myself beautiful now when I look at my baby pictures. I see my glistening eyes, my round head, my soft skin. I see myself as a cute child posing in a favorite dress, my smile lit by this simple joy. I see myself as a teenager with long auburn hair and freckles on my nose, and I see a pretty girl, the girl I never saw in my own mirror.

I can see myself now, and I was like every other girl. I was born a beautiful, loveable child like every other girl.

This is how I know you are beautiful. You are like every other person, every other human being alive on this Earth. You were born lovable. You were born beautiful.

Look into the mirror. You are beautiful!

Love,
Karen

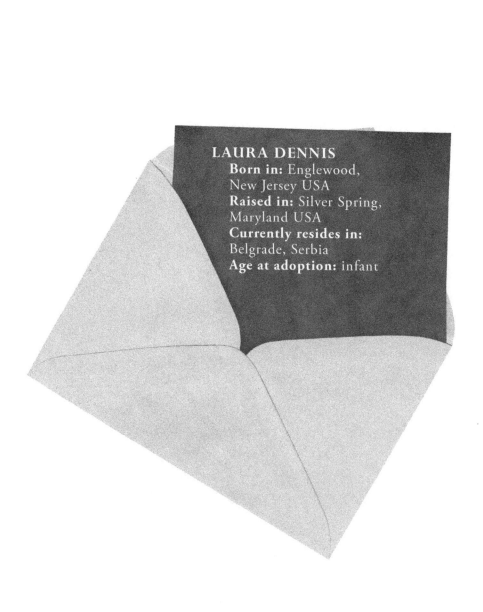

LAURA DENNIS
Born in: Englewood, New Jersey USA
Raised in: Silver Spring, Maryland USA
Currently resides in: Belgrade, Serbia
Age at adoption: infant

Dear Wonderful You,

I'll tell you a secret… my birthday is August 19.

I always hated celebrating my birthday as a child. I thought it was because it was a sad day. No one was around, what with family and friends being on vacation before the start of the school year. So why even have a party?

But the one birthday I looked forward to was my 18th.

There was something about turning 18 that made me think that my life was going to change. I thought that it was normal to feel this way, as most of my peers had similar angst and frustration towards— as we liked to call them, our "parental units."

Our "parental units" annoyed us to no end, they didn't "get" us, and they were always coming up with all these rules and dumb ideas.

All of which is a normal stage for teenagers, both biological and adopted.

But what I did not realize at the time was that my sense of who I was, in relation to my parents, was different, *precisely because* I'm adopted. The idea that my life was going to change when I became "of age," was specific to my "adoptee" status.

What do I mean by this?

Thoughts on Turning 18

I grew up in a closed adoption, with only a piece of paper about my biological background and the sentimental assurance that my birth mother loved me enough to give me up. (*How does that even work? How can you love someone so much you give them up?* Better to have said, "She loves you *in spite of* having given you up. We may not know the whole story right now, but we do know that it was not your fault.")

I was told that when I turned 18, my records at the adoption agency would be unsealed, and I would be able to access the name of my birth mother. I would be able to meet her, if I chose to do so.

Accordingly, my adolescent mind believed that *everything would change* when I turned 18. My life up until age 18 would be rendered somewhat meaningless; as I anticipated that I would somehow magically revert back to "The Person I Really Was Supposed to Be." In preparation for this birthday moment, I figured the most important things I could do would be to make myself the best, most successful, most perfect person possible. The idea being, I'd be perfect and ready to meet my birth mother.

More to the point, I'd be *worthy* of meeting her. I'd be worthy of her love, the love that she had and still held ... the love that inspired her to give me up in the first place.

Senior Year of High School

In my teenage mind, I deduced that the best way to ensure a successful life—which would begin with an amazing reunion—was to get straight A's and to be accepted into the best possible college. Senior Year, it all came down to Stanford University. Once I got in, I was absolutely SURE that I would be worthy of meeting my birth mother.

Certainly I was loveable if I was attending one of the best colleges in the country.

What better way to reinvent myself, as the real person that I truly was (not the adopted person that I'd grown up as) ... than to go away to college in hippie-dippy Northern California, 3000+ miles from my conservative, suburban Maryland hometown?

Graduation was in June, and I was "over it." I had no intention of keeping in touch with anyone; I was so bent on getting the heck out of Dodge.

July was spent working, saving money for college. (I'd been assured by my parents they'd send me to any college I got accepted to).

The month of August was spent picking out sheets and deciding what clothes to bring.

August 19 came and went.

The Rug Pulled Out from Under an Ill-Conceived Plan

My 18th birthday went unnoticed, forgotten.

Right around that time, my parents finally revealed to me that they could not afford even one quarter (like a semester) at Stanford.

"So what would be the point, Laura? The best thing we can do right now is to see if you can get into a local school."

It may sound spoiled to admit, but I was devastated.

Of course, not all parents have enough money to send their kids to such an expensive school. But the thing was, I'd put all my eggs in this one basket. I'd banked on reinventing myself completely at college—right down to my very essence, the definition of myself as a person.

I'd planned on not being adopted anymore.

Looking back on it, I think I subconsciously intended to reunite and become a completely different person; someone whom I actually liked, someone who didn't have to try to be perfect all the time.

Being Myself is Enough

It took me many years to realize: I had to confront those deep, self-hating parts of myself, and to accept that I *was always* good enough. I was always wonderful enough to reunite with my mother. She was always waiting for me, and she never expected me to be perfect. Far from it.

I still don't like celebrating my birthday, but I no longer feel ashamed to admit this reality. Not all adoptees feel this way, but for me, I don't like to celebrate my birthday because that is the day that I lost my mother. I lost her for not just 18 years, but for 23 years. Five years longer than necessary, because I felt ashamed that I'd achieved nothing in my life. I felt that because I didn't go to Stanford, I had no proof that I'd been given away to have a "better life."

Instead, it turned out that by being adopted, I simply had a different life.

Today I can say that I love my adoptive parents, I love my first mother, and I cherish the family I have created (husband and two non-adoptive kids). But it took me a long time to get there; too long.

Even though we were adopted, even though we *are* adopted, we are worthy of the love we have from our adoptive parents. And we are worthy of the love that we have from our first families—whether or not we are in an active relationship with them.

I might not have believed this "worthiness" mumbo-jumbo if someone told me it at the time. But then again, I only knew one other adopted person growing up, and he had absolutely no interest in his first family.

Perhaps if I'd had the opportunity to read this letter from my older (and wiser?) self, it would have connected with something deep within me. Perhaps I would have realized that I could relax, let go. Perhaps it would have dawned on my teenage-self that the person that I believed I could be, the person that I *wanted* to be, was exactly the person that I *should* be. No more, no less.

Warmly,
Laura

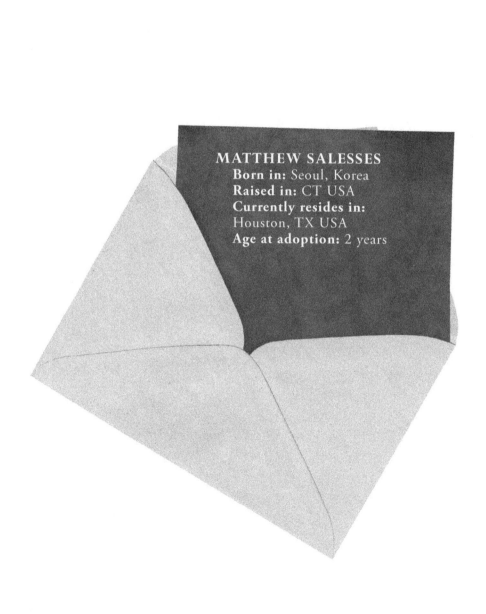

MATTHEW SALESSES
Born in: Seoul, Korea
Raised in: CT USA
Currently resides in: Houston, TX USA
Age at adoption: 2 years

Dear Someone Like Me,

LET'S START HERE: I WAS adopted, when I was 2, from an orphanage in Seoul; I am now 31; I married a (native) Korean woman; I have a 2-year-old birth child. Recently, my wife and I got into a fight during which she said, "I did not abandon you. I'm not your mom."

This was on a family trip to New Orleans, where neither of us had been before. We were spending the weekend with my adoptive parents, who had gone back to the hotel. We were fighting in the middle of a street in the French Quarter and my wife was pushing our sleeping toddler in her stroller as we shouted.

In the middle of the argument, my wife took off and left me standing by a bicycle pole. She blended into the crowd. I waited very bitterly. When she called about a half hour later, I didn't answer at first. I was still in the same spot. When I answered, I said, "You left me. You abandoned me."

I was being dramatic, of course, but I didn't mean anything related to adoption. I don't think. I meant abandoned in the plainest sense of the word.

When my wife came back, full of anger, that was when she said she wasn't my "mom." That was when I *felt* abandoned, as I stared at my wife who had these words lipsticked onto her mouth. I felt the fact of my adoption acutely.

I had sprained my foot the day before, so all I could do was limp away from her. I was so desperate for someone to talk to that I called my mother, but I couldn't say anything. I ended up staying away from everyone, not answering my phone, until after sunset.

It was the toddler who made me come back. My wife texted me that my daughter was asking where I was.

When I got back, my mother said this was just like when they drove me to college. I don't remember running off then. But, to be honest, there were plenty of times when I ran away from myself when I was younger. I guess I don't remember them all.

I sat my wife and mother down. My mother made the conversation about adoption right away, and I did my best to save her feelings while trying to explain mine. When I was younger, I never tried to save my parents' feelings. I just wanted someone else to experience as much hurt and confusion as I did. Now, when I better understand that feeling, when I can almost express it, I can't tell the whole truth because I don't want my mother to be sad.

My wife, and my mother, kept asking how they could make me "better." How to fix the problem of my adoption. But the basic problem is that my adoption was always supposed to be a solution unto itself. I had been taught to think of it as a solution, and what solution is there to a solution? It wasn't seen as a problem from the start, and now it is too late: one can't un-sink the boat and return to the point at which trying to make it a submarine seemed like a good idea.

Here is the problem they would make out: It is that, since my daughter was born, I have realized how much I don't know about myself.

This is because of how much we know and don't know about her. Other parents see that their children's ears come from a great aunt, or her facility with language comes from an uncle. I have realized that I am so much the way I am because of two blank years, unrecoverable. My present actions have been determined, in part, by the actions of someone I will never know, during a time I cannot remember.

So why can't I get over that?

(It's not fair, I told my therapist recently, that when we become adults and finally might have control over what we do, so much of our decision-making process has been determined by what happened to us as children, when we were not in control.

We were talking about how I take a fight to its bitter end because I hate the idea of not knowing what might have happened. I'd rather know than stop fighting.)

With my mother and wife, I tried to explain what I have learned from the experiences of other adoptees, older adoptees, that my difficulties with adoption are not like an epiphany, a single change from a moment of insight, but a continually lifting veil coming off again and again. I tried to explain that it will take me a long time (forever?) to adjust.

My wife had latched onto the idea that I was "finding myself." But I did that. I went to Europe, to Korea, as young people go abroad. This is not about not knowing who I am today. This is about not knowing who I was, and the impossibility of not knowing that and yet knowing who I am now. This is about not knowing *why* I am who I am today. I believed my entire life that it was because of a certain set of variables, *nurture*, when it appears it is much more because of a different set. *Nature,* but not exactly.

"I fell in love with one person and now I'm married to another," my wife said.

I couldn't get them to understand. We patched things up by a sort of expulsion. We spent what we could and tried to go on with empty pockets. I carry a weight they do not believe in.

On the drive back to Houston, I was listening to a podcast called, "The Partially Examined Life," in which a group of people discuss philosophical concepts, this time Thomas Kuhn's philosophy of science as a series of paradigm shifts.

From Wikipedia (emphasis mine):

Kuhn made several notable claims concerning the progress of scientific knowledge: that scientific fields undergo periodic "paradigm shifts" rather than solely progressing in a linear and continuous way; *that these paradigm shifts open up new approaches to understanding what scientists would never have considered valid before* . . . Competing paradigms are frequently incommensurable; *that is, they are competing accounts of reality which cannot be coherently reconciled.*

It was during a discussion of the "Invisible Gorilla" YouTube video that I realized: this is what I am going through, a paradigm shift. This is why it is not a quick thing. In the gorilla video, the viewer is asked to count how many passes a team of people in white shirts make with a basketball. The viewer concentrates on getting this number, and at the end, the video reveals that while you were counting, a gorilla walked through the frame and you didn't even notice. Once this is revealed, of course, you can't watch the video without seeing the gorilla every time, without *looking for it*.

My entire life, until my daughter was born, until she made the gorilla of adoption visible, is what I am saying, I was concentrating on how to fit in with those white shirts. I was concentrating on what I thought my problem was: how could I make myself like all the others, how could I make myself the kind of person who could live a good life as an American in America, as I surely was? But now the video is not about the white shirts at all. It is about the gorilla (and was always about the gorilla) and will always be about the gorilla from now on, unless there is another shift coming.

In the podcast, the discussion moved on to talking about science not as trying to find out what the world is—that isn't what science experiments really do—but as trying to prove the world is the way the paradigm says it is. That is why we do proofs to show that the big bang happened and the universe is still expanding. When we find anomalies, we try to figure out how they fit into the system we believe in. It isn't until a new paradigm comes along that the anomalies, sometimes, are explained. With the introduction of a new paradigm comes a scientific explosion, as we try to figure out how all of the old anomalies and new discoveries fit the newly accepted paradigm. We fit our world to our worldview. It takes a lot of time and effort to make up the proofs, though the paradigm can be introduced in a single essay.

That is what I was doing: I was testing what I knew about myself in terms of the paradigm I had. But the old rules don't fit anymore. The material is the same, but the sense I made of it has been completely called into question, and I will spend the next whatever number of years, or decades, or forever, figuring out how all of me fits the paradigm that recognizes adoption at the center of it, beating its chest, instead of counting passes.

As a kid who ran away a lot, as a man who went to Korea and married a Korean woman, I have a lot to re-see as if I was seeing it for the first time. It is the most serious undertaking to understand that the reasons might be different than I had thought. Two paradigms cannot exist together. One replaces the other. This is what we deal with, as adoptees, the shock not of finding ourselves but of realizing that we have always been there, unfound because our concentration was elsewhere, something most people do not have to deal with because they didn't have their original paradigm taken from them.

Yours,
Matthew
—

Invisible Gorilla video:
http://www.theinvisiblegorilla.com/videos.html

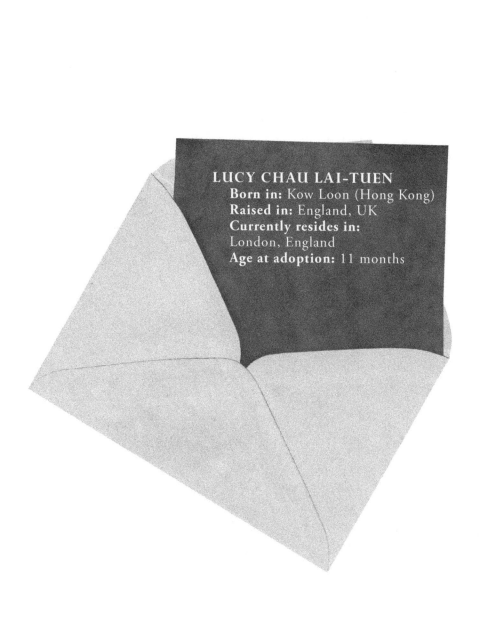

LUCY CHAU LAI-TUEN
Born in: Kow Loon (Hong Kong)
Raised in: England, UK
Currently resides in:
London, England
Age at adoption: 11 months

Dear Wonderful You,

THANK YOU FOR LETTING ME write to you. I hope that my letter gives some support, understanding, and perhaps a smile or even the odd laugh. It's not so much advice as well, just us having a chat. From one transracial adoptee to another adoptee, can I just say, you are not damaged goods. You are not "different" or any more different than anyone else is. We are all unique; we are all 'different'. In a conventional family where everyone is biologically connected, these "differences" are usually welcomed and celebrated. Because the norm is to identify with the same markers. The same facial features. This reinforces our belonging but at the same time we're always on the lookout for differences too. But when it comes to us adoptees somehow, "difference" throws us into a whole new ball park. With different rules and goal posts that never stay still. Don't ever lose sight of the fact that you are a person in your own right.

Many adoptees face unusual and complex challenges (lord knows there are thousands of blogs, websites, news articles and pieces on the internet to tell us this) over and above those that others do. But they should never be allowed to define and constrict us, which is what a lot of this language and terminology does. Don't allow others to use this as an excuse, or a reason why you can't . . .

So some of us suffer from mental health issues, so do many other people in society. I'm one of those people. I hit my late teens, had left home and had a nervous breakdown. Didn't realise I'd actually had one until a friend suggested that I see someone. I just couldn't stop crying and I really had no idea why.

Just because we may feel the need to talk through our concerns and fears, doesn't mean that we are acting out and it doesn't mean that we need to be institutionalised. It just means that we need someone to listen to us. And I mean really listen to us. Not just a nodding head.

Negotiating your way through life's ups, downs and even side-ways challenges isn't always "easy," it's not always going to be plain sailing and it's not always fun. But that's life for adopted and naturally born. As a transracial adoptee I had added extras to contend with like race, ethnicity, and identity to name the major and most important ones.

As a child I was not asking for special treatment. I just wanted someone to listen to me. Someone to talk to. Someone to reassure me that I wasn't actually loosing it. Back in the 60s in the UK, that was difficult. Well it was practically impossible. As a Chinese child brought up in a white, middle-class, conservative (for conservative read Democrat) area. I was the only non-white person in my immediate neighborhood. The only other "foreign" presence was an Indian Take-away. Not even a Chinese take-away. My adoptive parents had no connections to the Far East. They had hardly stepped outside of the area that they moved to when they got married. Which would have been a good ten years before they adopted me. Let alone travelling abroad. They passed the limited vetting procedures for adoption back in the late 50s and early 60s. Namely they owned property, they were of good character. Which meant they were able to get a Justice of The Peace, member of the clergy, Lawyer, Doctor or Policeman to sign an affidavit to that effect. Then bobs your uncle, you were approved.

I'm being slightly flippant about the process, even in the 50s-60s there was a little more to it than that, but not much. I was one of one hundred and six Hong Kong foundlings that were put up for transracial adoption to white families in the UK. (Hong Kong at the time being a crown colony of the UK). We were actually the first group of transracial adoptees that had ever been officially organised and adopted by UK families. The first time I dared to ask my adoptive Mother what the word adoption meant, I was physically reprimanded. I think it was the shock of hearing a six year old asking a question that my adoptive Mother didn't want to have to answer. Needless to say I learnt that lesson very quickly. I didn't ask about adoption again. When I eventually plucked up enough courage to ask about China; I was told that nosey, ungrateful, adopted Chinese children who asked questions were kidnapped by the Chinese and taken back to China. There I would grow up on a commune and be miserable. Needless to say I didn't ask any more questions about China either. I was petrified of being kidnapped. I had recurring nightmares well into my late teens. Navigating my way through the growing up process, dealing with all the usual challenges was bad enough but having to cope with the added extras?

I won't lie. There were many times when I felt so isolated that I might as well have been marooned on a desert island. I cried a lot on my own. I couldn't find anyone to talk to or who wanted to talk to me. The few friends that I did have, whilst sympathetic had no idea what I was talking about let alone what I was going through. When I was eighteen, I seriously thought about suicide. But I got through it, made it to adulthood and I'm still going. I'm sure you're probably sick of hearing "cute" or fancy phrases but it is true, 'It's always darkest just before the dawn,' even if naturalistically that is not the case.

The most confusing thing for me as a kid, teenager, young adult and even adult was my identity. Who exactly was I? What exactly was I? I was Chinese on the outside. But what was I on the inside?

I knew from a very early age because of the bullying and the beatings I got. Many children didn't see me in the same way as they did the white kids. There wasn't a day that didn't go by where some kid or adult didn't pull their eyes back as I passed. Call me a CHINK or yell at me in a fake Chinese accent.

"Ah so!" or "Me no spleakie Engrish."

That's when I needed my adoptive parents to step in, to stand up for me, to defend me. But they never did. I've suddenly remembered something. Must have been eleven or maybe twelve. I'd been taken to Paris. I can't remember exactly why, there would have been a reason, probably something to do with school. We were travelling on the Metro, a group of Parisian boys started taunting me, flicking my hair and calling me names. Trying to touch me. I couldn't speak French that well, but I knew what they were saying was not complimentary. My adoptive parents sat, stiff, rigid and very British, eyes front, ignoring me.

So I'm going to do it. I'm going to say to you what I wanted my adoptive parents to say to me. If anyone calls you names, makes fun of the way you look, the texture of your hair or the shape of your nose; don't ignore it. It's not nothing, it won't go away and if you tell an adult you're not being a snitch or a tattle-tail, you're helping to ensure another child doesn't have to suffer the pain and humiliation that you're going through. It's wrong, period. No one should behave like that. No one has the right to make you feel miserable, worthless, afraid or unhappy, just because you don't look like them. Just because you make them feel uncomfortable or uneasy. That isn't your fault. It's not your fault that they are idiots, ignorant or just plain stupid. It is unacceptable behavior. It's called racism.

Be proud of the way you look, the colour of your skin and the fact that your appearance is not the same as everyone else's. If everyone was the same, good grief, how dull and boring that would be. Never let anyone try and devalue you because your skin colour is different or your eyes are almond shaped. You are a human being, you have every right to exist and you are beautiful and amazing. Even if you don't realise it yet, you are, take it from someone who was an ugly duckling for over thirty years!

As I grew and became more self aware I wanted answers. I was curious. It's natural to want to know where you come from. How you fit into the world and those around you. My adoptive parents more often than not refused to answer any of my questions. I was met by a wall of stony silence. On the very rare occasions when one of my questions was answered it would be a short, terse reply. That was guaranteed to make me feel uncomfortable, as if I was doing something wrong. Let me assure you, if you receive this type of reaction from anyone, family, friends, peers or responsible adults, you are not doing anything wrong. The problem is with those that suggest you are. They are the ones that are "doing something wrong". These are the people that need to open their ears and listen to you. No one has all the answers, birth parents, adoptive parents, fosterers, adults we don't know everything but we have a duty to help and we can do this by just listening to you and being there for you.

Never be afraid to ask a question about your heritage, your

culture or your birth parents. If your questions are not answered then if you can, talk to an appropriate adult whom you trust. Talk to your closest friends, if they really are your friends they will support you and let you talk for as long as you want even if they can't really understand what it is you're going through. Because that's what it means to be a true friend. To listen, not to judge, not to project, but just to be there. If you come from a different part of the world where they don't speak English, then learn your native language. Having a second language is always a bonus, for work and for life. I'm over fifty years old. 2015/2016 I'm going to try and learn Mandarin (not that I haven't tried numerous times before) but I'm really going to try. Even if work does threaten to get in the way. Who knows— but I'll try. When I was growing up access to learning a non European language was practically zilch. Now there are so many ways you can learn and yes there's even an app for it! So if I can do it, so can you.

I'm still fitting the pieces together. Maybe I will never find all of them but that doesn't matter. What matters is that I know who I am and I'm proud of that. Yes, it's bitter-sweet, but there are so many huge pros. For a start I wouldn't be here writing this letter to you if I had not been adopted and I wouldn't have the diverse dual heritage that I have if I had not been adopted. Yes there are cons; I lost my family, being able to trace my roots. I lost the ability to speak my native language and I've grown up in a society that devalues people who are not Caucasian. I've been beaten up, I've lost work because I'm not white, because I'm not "Chinese" enough. I've been discriminated against by my own kind; I've been trolled and griefed by other adoptees who think that I shouldn't be speaking out. I'm still here. I'm not going to go away. I think what I think based on my personal experiences. The way that those memories made me feel, and how the choices made by others when I was a baby and child, made me what I am today.

Your story, your journey will be different from mine. But we will still share many commonalities. You have your entire life ahead of you. It will be exciting, perhaps sometimes scary and a little sad. But it is your journey. Your life and your discovery. I won't lie to you. Your life will be filled with experiences, joyous, happy, humorous, quirky, sad and some painful. But life overall is a wonderful journey, in spite of sometimes encountering negatives. You are on a journey literally of a life time that will lift you up in ways that you can't even imagine.

The first time I flew to Hong Kong was the first time I'd taken a long haul flight and it was in the days when flights had to stop over to refuel. It was a long grueling eighteen hours. But when I got to Hong Kong, I was so nervous it took all my will power to get myself out of my seat and walk off the plane. The landing hadn't helped. We landed at the old Kai Tak airport. That was terrifying passing through a maze of big high rises, being able to look into peoples' apartments and see everything. What struck me immediately once I'd landed was I looked like everyone else. I wasn't the odd one out. I realised then that I had spent seventeen years of my life looking down. Avoiding eye contact so as not to provoke or set someone off because my face was different from everyone else's. That was the silver lining. The dark cloud was the fact that I had never learnt to speak Cantonese. I'd asked, I'd begged when I was about eight maybe nine. I'd been told off. I'd be told that I was ungrateful and naughty for asking. I think I developed a slight complex about learning to speak Chinese after that.

The people that I met in Hong Kong were all very polite, very considerate to me when they found out my background. Many of them thought it was incredibly sad that I had lost my parents, my family. The Hong-Kongers treated me with much more sympathy and respect than many of the British East Asians back home had treated me. Most of who regarded me with suspicion, or open hostility because, as far as they were concerned, I wasn't really Chinese. I was a banana, yellow on the outside but white on the inside.

There are some (a minority) even now who still think of me as not being a real Chinese Person.

Whilst I was in Hong Kong for the first time I "felt at home." There were things that I instinctively know how to do. When I was taken to a temple for the first time I just automatically bought the joss sticks and bowed three times. I'd never set foot in a Buddhist temple before. I'd been raised in the Christian faith. My adoptive Mother was a Methodist. Central philosophical concepts that are entirely Eastern such as Wu Wei non-action or non-doing, were immediately accessible to me on a visceral level. It didn't need explanation. I just knew deep down inside what it meant and it was a natural, uncomplicated understanding. I can't explain it but there it was, I understood. I truly believe, as unscientific as it is, that there are some things that you just cannot take away from a person no matter what.

Of all the challenges I've faced, identity has to be the one that gave me, gives me the most pain. It's the one that still makes me cry inside. I feel it most when I go back to Hong Kong, or when I'm surrounded by Chinese people, who don't know me. It stings, it pulls and it cuts internally. You see I'm stuck between two very different cultures. It took me years to get used to that, to come to terms with it and be happy with the fact that I am at once both a child of east and west. The toughest part was accepting that not everyone would accept that or me. Learning how to live with that and be at ease is an ongoing process. It does get easier as you get older. The hard part was accepting who I was, the fact that I would never be completely whole. There will always be a bit missing from me.

I taught myself about China and the Chinese culture. I read every book, magazine and newspaper article I could about the China its history and culture. Which when I was a school child and young teenager was not a lot. Well in comparison to now.

Fifty years on and here I am, an actor, writer, filmmaker and transracial adoptee speaker and advocate. I wouldn't be doing what I do if I hadn't been adopted. Yes, there were some dark, unpleasant times. I cried a lot, I felt angry inside and I was lonely. But I managed to crawl my way through and here I am rambling on writing to you. I don't have all the answers. I just keep trying. Finally secure in my mixed up and incomplete identity.

"Since I was five, I've known that I was adopted,
which is a politically correct term for being clueless
about one's own origins." —Jodi Picoult

I hope that my scribbling has given you some comfort. If you have any questions please do write back, I'd love to hear from you.

Respect and kindest of regards,
Lucy

*"There is only one success - to be able to
spend your life in your own way."*

Christopher Morley

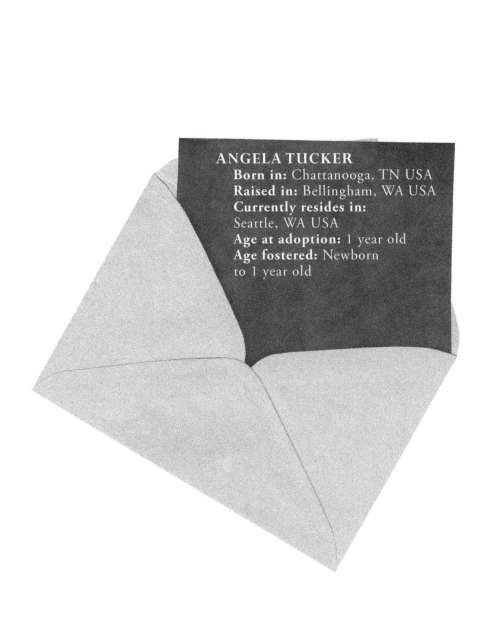

ANGELA TUCKER
Born in: Chattanooga, TN USA
Raised in: Bellingham, WA USA
Currently resides in:
Seattle, WA USA
Age at adoption: 1 year old
Age fostered: Newborn
to 1 year old

Dear Wonderful You,

YOU ARE A DIAMOND IN the rough. A crystal coalescing into something finer than diamond rings worn on people's left hand. You radiate with care for humankind, concern for wrongdoings and a zest for life. Because of this however, you are often weathered, exhausted and desiring a simpler life.

Strangers exhibit unabashed curiosity, asking private questions of you, such as—

"Where did you come from?"

"At what age were you adopted?"

"What happened to your *real* mom?"

These questions are an example of your effervescent sparkle, and evidence of others wanting to bask in your beauty, longing to understand the complexity of your shimmer.

Your sparkle is also present in the classroom. Your teachers may ask you to share about your ancestral heritage. Not knowing this answer may temporarily dull your glow. People wonder about your beaming smile and your enthusiasm, as they are perplexed as to how adoption and contentedness can go together. This is not your duty to share.

Although you shine wherever you go, you are also fragile – just like a crystal. The fragility of crystals is not a weakness. The sparkle of a diamond is not an invitation to steal. Your glimmering radiance does not entitle others to question you about where your sparkle came from.

We may not always see the stars twinkling brightly in the night sky, but we know they are up there. You too, can reserve your twinkle for whomever you choose; knowing that sometimes the cloud cover is so heavy that no one can see it. This is not accidental. We all need covering and warmth sometimes.

The word adoption often fractures me and creates ridges in my own crystallized self. I can feel my own shine dull when hearing others talk about adopting a pet. They speak of rescuing their dog which they found cold, wet, shaking and all alone wandering the streets. I see the "Adopt-a-Highway" signs on the side of the road and am curious about what that means. I wonder how my adoption might relate to adopting a road. As I think about this I notice my own sparkle becoming muted, the colors of my crystals change.

My own sparkle becomes muted, the colors of my crystals change. My shine loses its luster upon seeing the red squiggly line underneath the word; *adoptee* — signaling to me that the word has either been spelled wrong or the word does not exist. Even though I know it's spelled right and the word indeed exists. This is how some of my adoption fractures form.

Crystals take years to mature and sparkle, and go through many rounds of dulling and fading, becoming lackluster at times, and at other times being left to rest. For me, the dullness and rigidity comes from the sadness, fears, unpleasant reminders and constant peppering of insensitive questions. Your fragile moments and your happy moments will merge together to create your specific shine and shimmer. They will be a sparkling reflection of you and only you. This is what it means for a crystal to coalesce. This is why no two crystals are exactly alike.

You are a crystal, a diamond in the rough. This does not mean that you need to live your life on the mantle — displayed for all to examine every scar, break, color and jagged edge. Coalesce your sparkle by tending to your fragility.

Your friend,
Angela (A Fellow Coalescing Crystal)

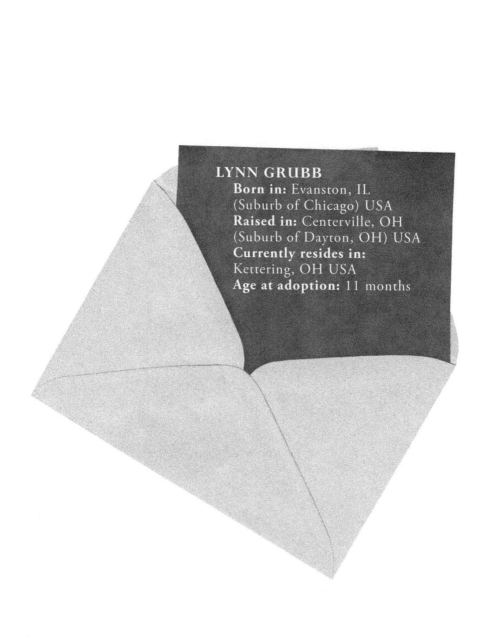

LYNN GRUBB
Born in: Evanston, IL
(Suburb of Chicago) USA
Raised in: Centerville, OH
(Suburb of Dayton, OH) USA
Currently resides in:
Kettering, OH USA
Age at adoption: 11 months

Dear Wonderful You,

WHAT ARE YOUR DREAMS? WHO do you envision yourself to be one day? Maybe these thoughts seem far away. Maybe you don't believe that you can do anything extra special in your life. I'm here to tell you that you can. You not only can, but if you start early, this love of that special dream in your life, will be carried with you into adulthood and beyond to the next generation.

Your long-ago ancestors have left their fingerprints on you, whether you know who they are or not. Little clues will show you the way. Are you inexplicably drawn to the piano? Do you feel a tug when you think about running in a marathon? Is there a whisper inside of you begging to be expressed on paper?

Are you tall? Are you athletically built? Do you have long fingers? Does music make you want to dance till dawn? Are you a computer geek? Do mystery novels excite you? Do you love insects?

The loves of your life will show themselves to you in your early years. All you have to do is pay attention. When I was in 4th grade, I was drawn to the violin, never knowing music was a legacy in my family of origin. Playing the violin led me to many rewarding experiences throughout my childhood, including being a member of the school orchestra and the Junior Philharmonic. I continue to share my love for the violin with others. Playing the violin also led me to an even greater love of mine, playing the keyboard.

Who would have thought that Jeff Kinney, author of *Diary of the Wimpy Kid* series, could do what he loved for a living? From childhood, Jeff loved to draw stick figures and now his books are loved by children and grownups everywhere, including this author.

Notice what sparks an interest inside of you and say "Yes" to that love in your life. You can say yes to an activity even if you do not have the money for lessons or teams. You can check out a book at the library. You can ask a friend or family member for help in finding resources. You can practice and study on your own. As long as you pay attention to the seed planted inside of you and begin taking steps toward realizing your dream, you will begin to build a foundation for your life.

Grownups are really just over-sized kids. We still have our own dreams inside of us. Writing this letter to you was one of my dreams realized. If you are struggling to find the gifts within you, never give up!

All my best,
Lynn

KAYE PEARSE
Born in: San Francisco, CA USA
Raised in: Indiana and
then Connecticut USA
Currently resides in:
Mid-Atlantic USA
Age at adoption: 1st
adoption at 16 months/ 2nd
adoption at 11 years old

Dear Wonderful You,

YOU KNOW WHAT WAS REALLY hard? I mean *really* hard? For me, it was when I was adopted and was told it would be "forever" and the people who adopted me would always be my parents. But then something changed and I discovered "forever" didn't mean *always* because those "forever" parents suddenly weren't my parents anymore.

Let me explain...

It happened to me when I was 10 years old. I'd been adopted as a toddler by an older couple. When my adoptive mother died my adoptive father decided he wasn't able to take care of me anymore. So he sent me to live with family members, and they officially adopted me about a year later.

So, yeah, I had a home and a family, but it was really *really* hard. I had to go to a new state, live in a new house, and have new people in my life whom I now had to pretend were my family. I had to figure out how to tell everyone at my new school why I suddenly showed up in the middle of the semester. I also had to change my name.

But the hardest part was trying to understand why this was happening. I mean, I knew my adoptive mother had died, but did that mean my father had to give me away? Remember, this was a repeat performance. First, my birth mother gave me away, and then my adoptive father gave me away. I truly felt like I'd done something wrong and it was my fault; that this happened because I just wasn't a lovable kid. After all, if my mom and my adoptive father really loved me, they would have kept me, no matter what. Right?

I was very confused, and I was very angry, and I was very depressed. I was full of grief over all my losses, and spent many nights crying myself to sleep. My new parents told me to "buck up" and "get over it" and didn't do anything to help me cope.

So I helped myself the best I could. I started writing poetry. It was really bad poetry, but since I was writing it just for me, that was OK. It helped just to put words on paper, and to give my thoughts a voice. I also threw myself into my music and would spend hours playing my guitar. And I read books. Voraciously. I'd wander through the school library looking for the biggest books and those were the ones I checked out and read. I loved losing myself in the stories of other peoples' lives and would often imagine myself living their adventures.

What I didn't do was talk to anyone about how I was feeling or what was going on my life. It was hard for me to make friends and, honestly, who wants to talk about stuff like that with another 10-year-old? And back then (this was a long time ago), there weren't the kind of services in school that are available today. Even if there had been, I was so convinced that I was an awful person that I probably wouldn't have asked for help anyway.

But you know what? That's just not true. The bad events in my life didn't happen because I'm a bad person, and they weren't my fault. And they're not your fault, either. I deserved stability and a permanent, loving, family, and so do you. If you haven't found a trusted someone to talk to about what's going on, please do, because that will help you make sense of it all.

Even though I don't know you personally, here's what I do know about you. You're a strong person. Maybe not physically, but definitely emotionally. While your adoption might affect you, it doesn't define you. You are smart and capable.

Above all, please believe me when I say that, no matter what's happened, there's nothing wrong with you. You are not a bad person. You're important, you have value and, yes, there is a place for you in this world. You and me? We were "chosen" – not to be adopted, but to have great depth of character.

I believe in you, and am excited about all the great things you're going to do.

Much love, from a fellow survivor,
Kaye

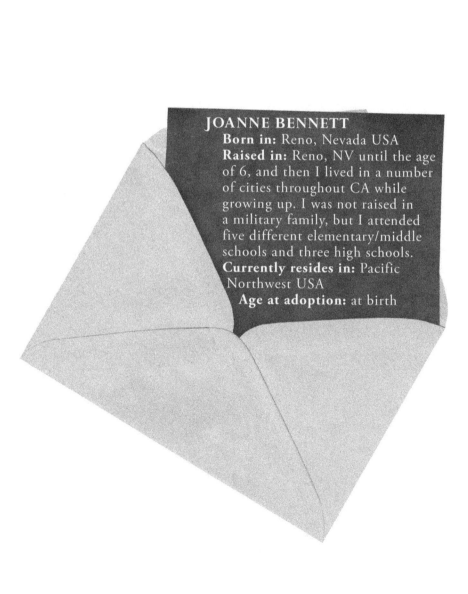

JOANNE BENNETT
Born in: Reno, Nevada USA
Raised in: Reno, NV until the age
of 6, and then I lived in a number
of cities throughout CA while
growing up. I was not raised in
a military family, but I attended
five different elementary/middle
schools and three high schools.
Currently resides in: Pacific
Northwest USA
Age at adoption: at birth

Dear Wonderful You,

DURING THOSE TIMES WHEN YOU struggle to see your beautiful reflection looking back at you in the mirror,

I WILL: say out loud — I matter; I am worthy of being loved.

I WILL: keep speaking kind and gentle words of affirmation to "me," that person in the mirror when I am feeling unsure of myself.

I WILL: try to remember that when adults in my life have let me down, that no child is to blame for the adult's weaknesses or failures.

I WILL: honor and respect my individuality, while always striving to be true to myself.

I WILL: confide in a trusting adult role model to ask for help when my life feels like it's spiraling out of control.

I WILL: find a way to not bury my deep feelings of being insignificant or of little value by writing in a personal journal.

I WILL: keep reaching for my dreams and know that each one of us has gifts, whether it's art, music, drama, or sports ... the list goes on.

I WILL: work towards never sucking up my feelings and emotions as a way of pleasing an adult role model, or with the belief that it might make someone love me.

I WILL: try to conquer my fears and negative thoughts with the help of my school guidance counselor, a therapist, crisis counselor or reading specific self-help books on adolescent issues.

I WILL: regardless if it's a peer or an adult, if anyone bullies or harms me in any way sexually, verbally, or emotionally, I vow to immediately report this abuse to someone of authority.

I WILL: know it is okay to have a place in my heart where it still feels safe to love my birth parents, even if they are not able to be there for me physically or forever.

I WILL: learn to love again ... freely and unconditionally.

I will begin to see that who I am on the inside is what is most important in life – not my body image, amount of material possessions, who has the most friends, or who is the prettiest or smartest. This is the true definition of what it means to become a healthy, successful human being.

Take care my friend,
JoAnne

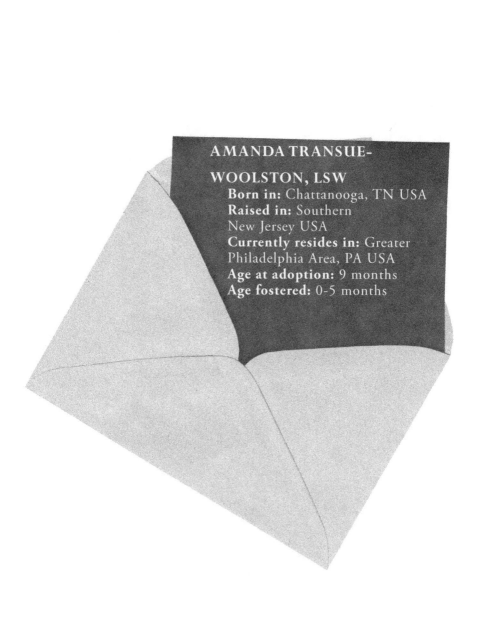

AMANDA TRANSUE-WOOLSTON, LSW
Born in: Chattanooga, TN USA
Raised in: Southern New Jersey USA
Currently resides in: Greater Philadelphia Area, PA USA
Age at adoption: 9 months
Age fostered: 0-5 months

TAKING HOLD OF THE PEN THAT WRITES MY LIFE STORY

Dear Wonderful You,

F OR AS LONG AS I can remember, I have had a number of memories
that make me say "ouch" when I think about them. Yes, "ouch,"
as in, "this hurts my head to even remember this." Maybe you have
those kinds of memories too. Memories of when I felt embarrassed,
rejected, or like things were spiraling out of control make my nose
scrunch up and a shallow feeling build in my stomach. *Why am I even
thinking about this right now?* I ask myself. What's the point, we can't
go back in time and change difficult parts of our life story, right?

Or can we?

Yep. You've read that right. I think we can go back and re-do
embarrassing, rejecting, out-of-control moments. As I have grown
older, I've realized that the pen writing my life story is in my hand.
This means I get to be in charge of my story and that I get to approve
what is written about me within my story. It means that who I think
I am and how I feel about myself in my life story are important. It
means I get to decide what my experiences mean to me, and that
I can even change those conclusions later in life if it feels right to
me. How do I do that? Let's visit one of my embarrassing, rejecting,
out-of-control memories and you can see what I mean.

It was history class in sixth grade. My teacher, posed a question
to the class about the lesson that day, and I can't quite remember
what she asked because I was so *mortified* by one boy's answer.

"It's because Amanda is UGLY!" he laughed, pointing directly at
me. The rest of the class laughed with him. They laughed *at* me.

I froze in my seat. I felt my face grow red and my palms begin to
sweat. My lungs burned with need for air, yet I feared drawing another
breath would trigger a cascade of tears. I looked at my teacher who
did nothing but roll her eyes at the laughing students and attempt

76

to move forward with the lesson. I was bullied by this boy every day. *Every single day.* Teachers did little about it, and no one was going to help me now. My mind began racing, searching for a route to escape this situation. Laughter surrounded me.

"I have to go to the bathroom" I said, instantly shooting up, straight-legged from my seat neglecting to smooth down my stiff, plaid uniform jumper.

I heard my teacher begin to protest my hurried departure from the room. I ignored her. *She can't keep me safe,* I thought to myself.

After fleeing down the long hallway, I pushed open the tall, beige door to the bathroom. My Mary Jane shoes pressed against the floor that was made of tiny green tiles with its old grouting crumbling ever so slightly. I stood in front of the mirror and examined myself. My blunted bangs. My shoulder-length, chestnut hair. My pale pink skin. My eyes a kaleidoscope of brown and green. *Is this what ugly looks like?* I wondered to myself. *It must be.*

The school secretary poked her head into the bathroom. I was in trouble. *Again.*

For a long time, I would feel ashamed and embarrassed whenever this memory would come to mind. Growing up, I saw myself in this story as ugly, as a troublemaker, and as unworthy of advocacy. I don't remember a time when I did not have an overwhelming fear of being rejected, and being bullied made this fear worse. And although the bullying stopped when I was a teen, my fear of being rejected, the shame I felt from being bullied, and the negative way I saw myself meant I wound up in relationships as a teen that weren't healthy and certainly didn't help me see myself in a positive way. Memories like these from the tough parts of my life story *hurt.*

But remember I said that I think we can re-write these stories? I can't rewrite what actually happened, but I can rewrite my role in the story. I can write a better way of seeing myself. A more *accurate* way of seeing myself.

Looking back on the memory now as an adult, it still hurts a little. However, it no longer affects the way that I see myself. I am not, nor have I ever been ugly. *No one is.* No one should define beauty for anyone else. I was not a troublemaker. The way I reacted to being bullied often got me into trouble. I was a child who was being mistreated by peers, and this did not make me a bad person. I am, and always have been, worthy of being advocated for. *Everyone is.* My emotions and my sense of safety are important. I am important because I am human.

I once saw myself within my adoption story as someone who was *unwanted.* When I took hold of the pen that writes my adoption story, I knew I could not rewrite the history that lead to my surrender to foster care and then adoption. Yet, I could write that I was worthy of being wanted and that I am worthy of love and care. *Because I am and so are you.*

Thinking differently about myself when recalling the memories that make up my life story has become easier as I've grown older and have developed new thinking skills and ways to think better thoughts about myself. Practicing thinking good thoughts about myself lets me look back at my life story and feel good about the positive memories that I have. The good memories are a source of strength for me and thinking about them makes me feel happy.

Taking control of the pen that writes your story isn't just about writing an actual story like I did here in this letter, but any way you choose to express yourself. The American rapper, Eminem, writes his story through song. In 2002, he released a song about his childhood abuse called *Cleaning out my Closet.* His song was intended to cut ties with his mom, and in the music video an actress portrayed his mom flipping through letters that said "I hate you" in big letters. Twelve years later, he rewrote this story and released a new song called *Headlights.* None of the historical events of his abuse or witnessing his younger brother be placed into foster care changed. What has changed is how he *sees himself* in the story. He rewrote himself as someone who is older and wiser, and who has grieved his losses. He understands that he deserved a better childhood. He tells his mother that he forgives and loves her, but not because the bad things that happened to him as a child were OK. In this story, it seems that *he needed* to be able to love her and forgive her. I can't make meaning of Eminem's story for him. However, my interpretation of his art from the outside looking in, tells me that rewriting his story and drawing new conclusions about his mother is a source of incredible strength *for him*.

Taking control of the pen that writes our life story sounds pretty intimidating at first, doesn't it? Here's the thing, being in charge of our story doesn't happen all at once for three big reasons that I can think of. First, we start in life learning a lot of our story from others. We learn about our family history through stories family members tell. Our adult caregivers tell us our stories from when we were too young to remember. For those of us who had multiple caregivers, caregivers we've never met, or foster care or adoption files that we've never seen, collecting our stories is a big job that takes time. Even if you don't know your entire life story from the beginning you still get to be in charge of it.

Second, not everyone responds to our story in ways that are nice or that respect that we are our story's rightful tellers. It hurts when those around us, especially those close to us, can't accept our story. I know when I was younger feeling my story was not accepted by others made me not want to tell it to anyone.

Third, young people don't focus on their story, especially hard memories, all the time. One of my favorite educators, Dr. Shapiro, calls it "dipping in and out of grief." One day, a young person might focus on a sad part of their story, another day they might focus on a happy part, and then for a while they might not focus on their story at all. Sometimes if you've spent time thinking about something sad and move on to think about something happy, our story listeners may feel frustrated when we return once again to the sad memory later. Even supportive people have a tough time realizing that working on a life story is a process that doesn't focus on one single feeling all the time.

It took me a long time to feel as though I was truly in charge of my story. It came to me through a series of small steps. I asked friends and family members to share memories about me from times I could not remember. I read my adoption and foster files that I could gain access to. I collected pictures of ancestors and childhood memories. I wrote in a journal. I shared bits and pieces of my story with others. I gathered story listeners around me, friends and family who knew my story would have sad and happy parts and accepted it. I practiced telling my story until I felt strong.

This is what rewriting our stories and this letter is about: *strength*. It's about telling you that there is strength within you. It's about picking up the pen that writes our story so we can write about how strong we are. I cannot tell you what conclusions to draw about your own story. Every person and story is unique and every person is entitled to make meaning of their own story for themselves. There is also no one right way of thinking about being adopted or fostered. However, I do think that one thing is *always* true. For those of us who were adopted and fostered as youth, our lives and stories have value. We have value because we are human and we deserve for this truth to be reflected in the story we tell of our lives. This is how, without knowing you, I can address this letter as *Dear Wonderful You*. Because— **you are wonderful**.

With admiration and respect,
Amanda

BRENDA M. COTTER
Born in: Springfield, MA USA
Raised in: West Springfield, MA USA
Currently resides in: Newton, MA USA
Age at adoption: 4 months

Dear Adoptee,

I AM CURRENTLY 58 YEARS OLD and I am both an adoptee and the parent of two girls adopted from China. I have thought about adoption issues and my identity as an adoptee all of my life. My perspective has changed over time as I matured, as attitudes and adoption policies have evolved, when I met my birthmother and birth family, and when I became a parent.

I was adopted when I was four months old in May 1956 in West Springfield, Massachusetts. When I was three years old, my mother told me that I was adopted. I have a vivid memory of it. She told me that that my parents "chose" me and that was very special, but she also told me never to tell anyone and that if I did, people would treat me differently. Of course, I did not understand this profoundly mixed message at the time. But, it left me with a shadow of fear and shame connected to this unspeakable secret. Worse, when I was about 8 years old, I broke the taboo and told my best friend that I was adopted. Somehow my mother overheard and, unbeknownst to me, went to my friend's mother the next day and told her that I made this up and it was untrue. My friend's family, to whom I was very close, simply would not believe me when I told them and insisted on the truth.

My parents' attitudes were driven by the times. In the 1950s, adoption was not viewed as a positive alternative, but as a second-class way to build a family. When I was adopted, my birth certificate was changed to read as if my parents' had given birth to me and that fiction reflected the attitudes of everyone in the adoption process. My parents were told that I was now theirs and my past was a closed book, never to be investigated or reopened by anyone.

Of course, I was a curious kid. Before I feel asleep at night, my mind would travel to all kinds of mysteries: the universe, the concept of infinity and my own past. I had a million questions but I also accepted, the way children do, that the answers were unknowable. But that impenetrable and essential mystery, fundamental to my identity, felt like a deep hole inside of me. My parents made it very clear that my questions were unwelcome. In retrospect I see that based on what they were told and understood, they viewed my questions as an indication that either something was wrong with them or something was wrong with me. I quickly learned to keep my thoughts to myself.

In view of the secrecy, I grew up feeling like I was the only adoptee in the world. This changed one day in the early 1970s when I heard about an organization called "Orphan Voyage" that was bringing adoptees together to talk about their experiences and advocate for more openness. I ventured into a meeting in Boston and, for the first time, encountered other adoptees. There were about 30 people there sharing their experiences about when they learned they were adopted (many only learned as adults) and, in many cases, their search for their birth parents. This meeting was transformative for me. I cannot even put into words the relief and excitement I felt to learn that many others shared my feelings. That group also recommended a book to me by Dr. Betty Jean Lifton called Lost and Found. Dr. Lifton was a well-regarded psychologist, adoptee and, ultimately, major advocate for adoption reform. That meeting, and reading about Dr. Lifton's remarkable and insightful journey, marked a major turning point for me. I no longer felt that adoption was a part of my identity that dare not speak its name. I began to actively look for information and connection.

In my late 20s, I decided to search for my birthmother. I considered moving the Court to unseal my records and by luck and circumstance I was introduced to a wonderful lawyer in Cambridge, MA who also happened to be an adoptee. She advised me that while the records were supposed to have been sealed, Springfield was a little behind the times and I probably could find my adoption record in the archives. She was right. I also had a little help from the agency from which I was adopted. I met with a social work there and she told me that they could not release any information to me except non-identifying general information. But then she brought the file into a private room with me, slid the file to the middle of the table, looked me in the eye, and told me she had to leave for a meeting for about 15 minutes. She left me with the file. I now had my birthmother's name and ultimately, with a little more detective work, her married name, address and phone number.

I sent a note to her saying that we had met briefly in the 1950s and I wondered if she remembered me. I crafted the note so that only she would know its meaning. She called me immediately and we followed that with a meeting shortly thereafter. I met her daughters and also, through her, was able to locate and meet my birthfather's family (he had died). These meetings were surreal. I could not believe that I was looking in the face of biological relatives: my mother, sisters and brothers. My birth father's family had a gap tooth smile like me and I learned about my birth father's intense temperament-so similar to my own.

Make no mistake. I was not looking for a new family. I always had perfect clarity that my parents were my adoptive parents. My father is not my "adoptive" father, he is simply my dad. Whereas, my biological father always gets the qualifier. My birthparents gave me a genetic heritage, nothing more and nothing less. But that genetic heritage was of critical importance to me. Solving that mystery filled that indefinable hole inside of me and made me feel whole as a person. And, while I liked the genetic relatives that I met and felt a deep connection to them, my immediate thought when I met my birth family was this: I am so grateful that everything happened as it did. I realized in one of the most important insights of my life that I would never choose a different path. While there are profound losses inherent in adoption, if everything had not happened as it did, the acute losses would be on the other side-I would never have met all of the people, friends and family, teachers and mentors, that I held and hold so dear. That peace and gratitude have stayed with me. Along the way, I told my parents about finding my birth parents. I could see their fear dissipate when they realized that I was still, unquestionably, their loving daughter.

One thing I was absolutely certain of though. I wanted to have biological kids. I wanted the genetic connection to my kids that I did not have in my own family. And, I was sure-beyond any shadow of a doubt-that I would never adopt. It was just not for me. But life is funny. Thankfully sometimes life will point you in the right direction even if you have to be dragged kicking and screaming.

So, the best thing that ever happened in my life is that I am the parent of two beautiful daughters adopted from China. I adopted Charlotte when she was five months old and Laura when she was thirteen months old. They are now 19 and 18. My own adoption history has been a huge benefit in being their mom. I think they find connection in our common status as adoptees and I can understand and relate to many aspects of how they feel. The truth is that while each adoptee has her own journey no one can understand how it feels to be an adoptee, to be separated from one's genetic origins and connections, except another adoptee. But my children have experiences that are vastly different from my own in multiple dimensions. They are growing up in an interracial family and they have been separated not only from their genetic roots, but also their cultural roots. At the same time, they are growing up at a time when adoption is openly discussed and the Internet makes connections possible across the world. Each of my children has their own story, informed by their circumstances, as well as whom they each are. Charlotte has become fluent in Mandarin and started a worldwide organization to connect and provide mentorship and resources to Chinese adoptees. Laura has always been less interested in China and adoption issues, but she forged a profound and wonderful connection to her roots by volunteering with, and providing ongoing support for, Chinese orphans with special needs.

So, what words of wisdom and advice can I offer? First and foremost, listen to yourself and trust your own instincts. While there are some common adoption experiences and issues, everyone has their own story informed by their own inherent qualities and their life experiences. At the same time, if you are wrestling with issues related to your adoption, reach out. We have the amazing good fortune to live at a time when connections to others experiencing similar issues are often only a click away. However unique your story is or may seem, there are others who will relate to you and support you. Second, remember that adoption is complex and the truths and realities you may discovery for yourself are likely not going to be black and white or binary. Adoption entails losses and benefits and they exist together side by side. Who knew that my experiences, and the sometime painful yearning that I experienced as a teenager, would someday help me to be a better parent to my daughters? And, while this may sometimes be hard for your adoptive parents to understand, the desire to find and connect with your genetic heritage is natural (but not universal) and has little or nothing to do with your love for your family formed by adoption. Both can comfortably co-exist. Finally, although this may seem harsh, we cannot go back, only forward. Understanding our own history and identity is of the greatest importance but we must ultimately accept and embrace the present and the future.

For me, coming to terms with my identity as an adoptee has been a lifelong process. I have experienced it, in some ways as a blurry picture that has come into increasingly sharper focus over time. And, sometimes what has been revealed has taken me totally by surprise, including the fact that the adoption thread running through my life has been the source of much of its richness.

With warm regards,
Brenda

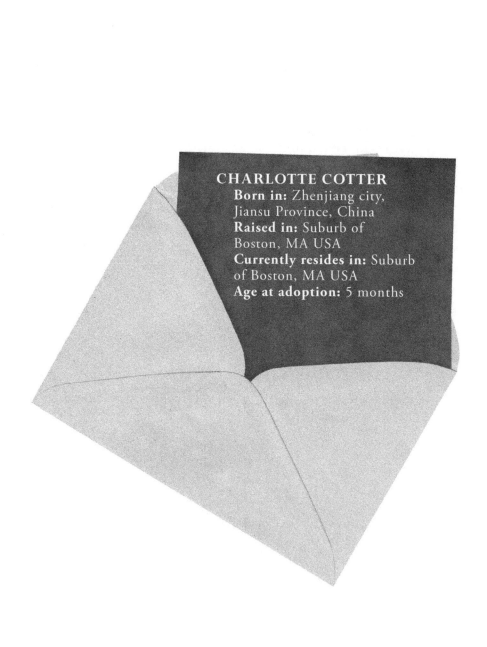

CHARLOTTE COTTER
Born in: Zhenjiang city, Jiansu Province, China
Raised in: Suburb of Boston, MA USA
Currently resides in: Suburb of Boston, MA USA
Age at adoption: 5 months

Dear Wonderful You,

MY NAME IS CHARLOTTE, AND I am 20 years old this year. This year, I will be a sophomore at Yale University, where I will be studying Chinese and East Asian Studies. I, of course, love China and studying Chinese, but I am also passionate about community organizing, empowering young leaders, and volunteering and service work. In my free time, I like hanging out with my two dogs and tap dancing.

I am also adopted. I was born in Zhenjiang city, Jiangsu province in August of 1994 and was adopted early 1995 at a mere five months old. My mom always used to say that I am 100% American and 100% Chinese. From the beginning, she encouraged me to embrace my Chinese roots, and often introduced me to other adoptees to hang out with. In retrospect, this exposure actually did benefit me greatly. But when I was young, I never really took to my Chinese side, or had any real interest in being adopted. It was just a passing thought that vaguely touched the sides of my consciousness.

In middle school, I was able to choose a language to learn. I originally wanted to choose French, but my parents encouraged me to study Chinese because they said I would one day appreciate it. This decision, and this is no understatement, changed the entire course of my life so far. I ended up falling in love with the beauty of Chinese language, the rhythmic sounds, the artistic characters, and the rich cultural history embedded within every phrase. It seemed to me at the time that I fell in love with Chinese not because I was a Chinese adoptee, but because of the inherent charms of the language.

During high school, my passion for Chinese took off– I lived and breathed Chinese. I ended up competing in national and international Chinese speech competitions, teaching Chinese classes for local adoptees, and even spending the last four months of my senior year of high school living and studying in Beijing. This intense commitment to Chinese sparked me to deeply rethink and re-evaluate my thoughts on adoption. I started to realize that, at some level, my interest in Chinese was indeed connected to my roots. How curious I had been about China, about Chinese culture, and about the world that I lost as an infant. How I longed to meet my birth mother and family, and yet how sad I had been that I would not have been able to communicate a single word. Maybe, I discovered, learning Chinese was an important step in reclaiming what I lost in the past, or if I think about it in a different way, actively creating opportunities where I can connect to China for the future. In any event, at the end of high school, I realized that being adopted had become an important part of my identity, and that I had deeply internalized my 100% Chinese and 100% American identity.

Then came the curiosity. I realized that I desired to meet and talk to other adoptees, and that, for the first time, this desire came from me and not my parents. I wanted to exchange stories and hear about their opinions on adoption, but I also wanted get to know them as people – their hobbies, interests, personalities, and passions. I talked a little about this with my mom, and we realized that the number of organizations for adoptees, and especially those created for adoptees and by adoptees, was little to none.

Together with my co-founder Laney, I set out to change that. In May 2011, Laney and I founded China's Children International, an online support and networking organization created by and for Chinese adoptees. Today, we have over 1,300 members.

Because of my involvement in China's Children International, I have had the opportunity to meet the most amazing, inspiring people, and I have gotten involved in many exciting, unique projects within the adoptee community. I have deeply felt the importance of community – it was as if China's Children International finally gave me that feeling of acceptance that I had long been searching for. I've also gained a new perspective on how I view my identity. I see myself as a global citizen, both American and Chinese, someone in a position to connect these cultures and peoples. It's a totally new identity, and one that I am intensely proud of. Although being an adoptee does not define who I am, being an adoptee is an extremely important part of my identity and of my personal journey so far, and something that I am immensely grateful for.

But I know that not everyone agrees with me. Some tell me that being an adoptee makes them feel as though they don't belong anywhere, and that they are constantly searching for that place of belonging. Some tell me that the pain of losing their culture and their heritage is so strong they wish they hadn't been adopted. Some would rather think that the past is in the past, so why bother with thinking about their adoption? These are all valid thoughts. Through this organization, I have learned of the incredible diversity within the so-called group of "Chinese adoptees." No two adoptees have the same opinions on adoption issues - and it is OK to have different thoughts on these issues, whether they are positive, or negative, or critical, or optimistic. It does not matter what any other adoptee says – your journey is your own, and if you feel it, it's your truth, so embrace it. In fact, for me, it's precisely this diversity of opinions that makes for such a vibrant community; hearing the varied voices of the adoptee community very often inspires me to re-think and re-evaluate what I thought I knew about adoption from many different angles!

Even with the support of the community though, no one ever said being an adoptee is easy. What I struggle with most is being good enough. When I was given up, I know it was probably because of the one child policy, the preference for boys over girls, and the economic struggles China was facing, but there is always that nagging doubt, what if I wasn't good enough? If that is true, what do I have to do to be worthy of keeping now? How hard do I have to work? How successful do I have to be? This is my largest struggle as an adoptee, so when I was writing this letter, I thought to myself, what would I say to someone in my shoes?

First of all, I want to let you know that you do not have to live your life trying to be good enough for the next person. All you need to know for yourself is whether you are trying being the best you that you can be – compassionate, kind, gentle, giving. Let the rest go. Trying to be so good all the time, you must be so tired. I understand how hard it is. I want to let you know that, no matter what, you are good enough. I accept you as you are, without needing to live up to any standards. You are innately beautiful inside and out. You deserve everything good that is ever coming to you and more. You can do amazing things, so much more than you have ever dreamed. You are loved. You are wonderful.

I wish you the very best now and forever.

Love,
Charlotte

JOE SOLL조 살, LCSW
Where were you born: Unknown
Where were you raised:
Nyack, New York USA
Where do you reside now:
Congers, NY USA
Age at adoption: at birth

CONFLICT OF TWO MOMS - AN ADOPTEE'S DILEMMA

Dear Wonderful You,

I AM WRITING TO YOU AS an older brother might write to his younger sibling.

I am adopted too and I want to tell you some things I've learned.

As adoptees we are usually socialized to believe we can only love one mother, yet we are told we are adopted and that our first mother couldn't or wouldn't keep us or is dead etc., and that is supposed to be the end of it. But it cannot be.

Babies are born loving the mother who gives birth to them. So, how could we not think about our first mother? Why can't we love both of our mothers?

Since to children growing up, their mothers are all powerful goddesses, children believe their mothers know everything. Therefore to an adopted child growing up, if they think about their first mom with love, their adoptive mom will know and may be angry. The adoptee knows that she lost her first family for some reason and doesn't want to be "re-abandoned" no matter what. So, the adoptee might feel she has to stop thinking about her first mom.

To complicate matters, if the adoptee thinks about her adoptive mom with love, her first mom will know and not return. All of the above is usually unconscious but causes a powerful conflict that is difficult to deal with. The feelings and thoughts get buried. When they are buried we may not even know they exist.

As we grow older and think about searching for our first mom, our thoughts of searching may well trigger the conflict of two moms and an inner battle of loyalty will often ensue. If I love this one, that one will "reject" me and vice versa.

So we are caught in the middle of this very powerful, emotional conflict. For the adoptee, the usually unconscious struggle seems like life and death. If I choose a relationship with my first mom over my adoptive mom, it might feel like a death. The fear can be terrifying and not logical. Some adoptees need additional help to conquer this fear.

Also, many adoptees have rage at their first mom for leaving in the beginning and cannot trust, no matter what they are told— that their mom won't leave again.

It is often an unconscious fear of being loved by our first mom that tips the loyalty scales towards our adoptive mom. This is not about whom one loves more but who is safer to one's inner self, an inner self who is terrified about being left again.

This conflict can be assuaged for us if we are willing to talk to a counselor about these feelings.

To further complicate matters, it's common for our adoptive parents to be terrified we will leave them for our first parents. So we need to reassure them and try to help them understand that we search not to replace parents but to know where we come from, to know our story.

Searching is healthy and normal. Adolescence is the time of identity solidification so the earlier one searches, I believe, the better; however, preparation before for searching is necessary.

For all involved— we need to understand that we adoptees can love two moms without lessening the love that we have for them.

I hope what I have written here will help you.

With caring,
Joe

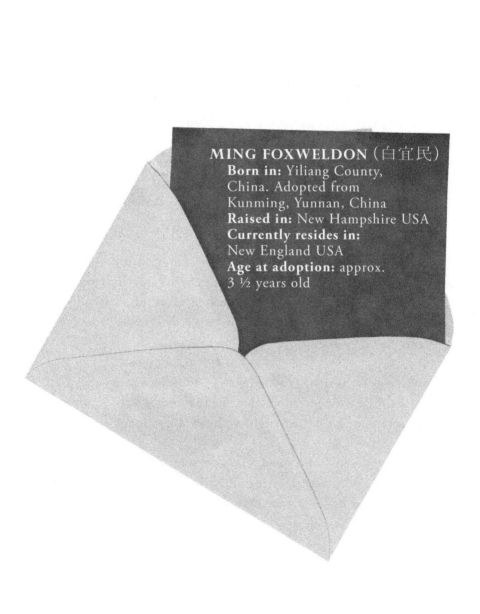

MING FOXWELDON (白宜民)
Born in: Yiliang County,
China. Adopted from
Kunming, Yunnan, China
Raised in: New Hampshire USA
Currently resides in:
New England USA
Age at adoption: approx.
3 ½ years old

Dear Wonderful You,

READY, SET, READ. FIRST, I want you to know something really important. "You Are Beautiful." I know this is a very simple phrase, but it's something I want you to never forget. No matter what anyone says to you, you are loveable, worthwhile, and your footprint matters. There will be storms you will have to ride through, and moments in which you wished could be erased. But know that what you have gone through in your life, makes you, you. I know I sound so simple in my speech, but I want you to know that you have so much to offer on your life journey. You define you, no one else. No matter the labels, the name-calling, etc. You are still you. I think it is important to question what comes in your life, whether it is from your parents, your friends, or your teachers. Anyone. It's only natural to wonder about your past, want to seek answers in your own way. If you are not interested to look into your past, that is OK. But know that can be something which teaches you. The present is important to recognize. The future is worth working for.

I want you to know that no matter where you are, you will be challenged. Sometimes these challenges will make you want to run away immediately. Other times you will want to face them head on, despite how hurt you may get. In the end it's your choice what you take away from these experiences. Even if you meet others who have shared a similar past as you have, they are still themselves, and you are you. As you grow up, and begin new chapters of your life, you will experience transitions which, at times, you will be afraid to face. There will also be times when you may feel excited and will move forward with enthusiasm. Just know it's OK to take a step back, and really analyze the situation, observe what you like about it, what you don't, and then make your decision. Taking risks is all about why each and every one of us is alive. It's why those who care and love us are alive.

There will be times in your life that you question everything about yourself. The things you say, do, write ...everything. It will feel like a whirlwind of chaos to clearly express yourself to the world. There will be challenging yet wonderful experiences— developing your identity, learning to expand your mind, getting to know yourself. I want you to know the road you are on, is unique. No one else will have an experience identical to yours— not even others who appear to share similar stories.

It can be scary at times, and there will be days you feel lost, hopeless and insecure. I assure you that you can pull through the rough times, and come back on top, a better, stronger and confident individual. Be patient with yourself, seek out those who truly care, love and respect you. Know that your story is yours to own. No one can make you tell it. You have a right as a human, to speak your mind however you want. There will be times when others will ask questions that will stop you in your tracks. Some experiences might make you want to crawl into a hole and hide. Or maybe it'll make you want to express yourself in ways you never felt you were capable of. Still, you and you alone have every right to feel what you feel. Acknowledge it. Whether that is through writing, singing, dance, sports, whatever your way of expression is, don't hesitate to go for it! Surround yourself with people who will be your cheerleaders and your role models. Keep them close to your heart and remember love can be expressed in a variety of ways.

I hope you will be courageous, however you see fit and go and pursue what your heart desires.

Dear Wonderful YOU,
First things, first
Continue being
Be-YOU-Ti-Full!
Never let anyone say otherwise
Those individuals
Who say and do things
To put YOU in a dark
Place
Don't pay any mind

Because
This is THEIR call
Shortcoming of some kind
However
YOURS
To call upon YOURESELF
Through persistence
TIME
ENERGY
YOUR MIND
Will YOU achieve such wondrous dreams
To follow YOUR heart
Create goals
Reach them
From school projects,
Winning a big game,
Attending that first dance,
Going on adventures,
Graduating,
Getting that dream job...
Whatever it may be,
Be proud
Know who YOUR friends are
Know that distance is OK
Though it may be hard to face
YOU have to seek out those who truly care
LOVE
YOU
Unconditionally
YOU tell YOUR story
No one can tell it
The end

YOURS truly,
Ming
(Traveler of Time)

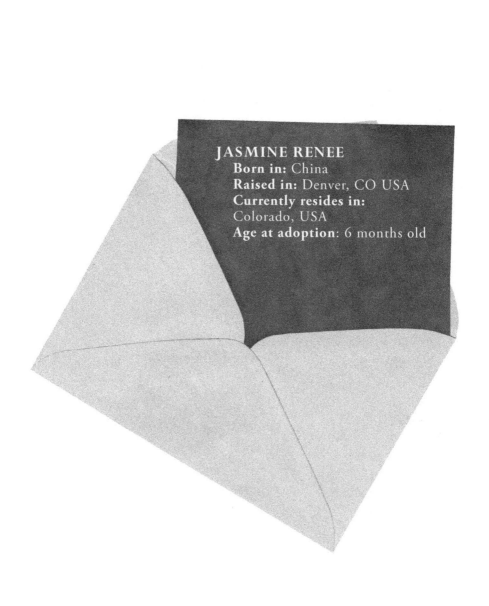

JASMINE RENEE
Born in: China
Raised in: Denver, CO USA
Currently resides in:
Colorado, USA
Age at adoption: 6 months old

Dear Young Philosophers,

I HAVE DISCOVERED MY NEW FAVORITE humanitarian, Joe Campbell, whom I recently came across in my language arts class. His sagacity has helped me on this journey of my last year in high school and I wanted to share some of his views with you, because they may help you in your journey.

"I don't believe people are looking for the meaning of life as much as they are looking for the experience of being alive."

I know you may have many questions about this life and your journey, which is simply a natural human characteristic. Although, you may have more questions, because when you were tiny, just one decision changed the whole outcome of your life.

It's amazing that some choices we make can have such a long-term affect. Sometimes these choices can lead to a tour de force or sometimes a quagmire. I've realized that adoption is something that you will ruminate over or passively ignore at times, which is fine. We all have our feelings and I do believe everything we feel is true and for a reason.

The only thing I worry is that you will drown in the grievance of unknown joys. Yes, not knowing your birth parents may dawn on you and you may feel a painful longing to know something about them. Although I am a person who believes things happen for a reason.

I realized it's important to open our eyes and be thankful for what's around us. I'm not going to use hackneyed statements like "You're lucky" or "you're better off here," because who knows, I mean how would anyone know that? There may be a good chance but regardless, remember to open your eyes to the beautiful loving people who have touched your heart through this journey.

Life is a paradox and who knows, maybe you will receive information about your parents one day and find out that they're some of the wealthiest people in China.

Although, for now just live in this moment and appreciate the moments you have now, because soon these moments will be gone and you'll regret not paying attention to the beauty and love brought out in those memories.

Growing up, you may be teased or asked profound things like "What's adoption?" "Do you know you're real parents?" "Are you Mexican?" "Is everything smaller because your eyes are so tiny?" My advice is it's your choice to answer honestly or not at all, but be sure to always maintain your integrity. People will ask questions because the idea of being "adopted" is a new thing to wrap their heads around. No matter what, stay true to yourself and your beliefs.

Life may be filled with trepidation at times and have you asking questions like "Is this really what life is about?" Yes life can be dark, but sometimes it's god-awful times like these that make us grow for the better. The times you feel vulnerable are the best times, because when you're feeling lost eventually you'll be found. Life isn't easy, but it's the way we choose to handle our quagmires that truly matters.

Joe Campbell also said, "It is by going down into the abyss that we recover the treasures of life. Where you stumble, there lies your treasure."

Words I will continue to live by my whole life.

Lastly, I want to say follow your passion. The bliss that truly fuels and sets fire to your soul. Although, with caution, never have your bliss be a selfish thing. Your bliss isn't supposed to come easily or right away or root from greed. It comes from hard work and passion. Follow your fervor and live life expressing love to others. The definition of love simply put is sacrificing your needs and self-restraints for the benefit of others, just because. You can follow your bliss and help others along the way.

Joe Campbell also said "Follow your bliss and the universe will open doors where there were only walls."

Remember it's the journey not the destination.

Keep these quotes with you not in your mind, but in your heart. I know you'll go far in life, even if it takes you in an unexpected direction.

Much love,
Jasmine

MAY SILVERSTEIN
Born in: Yiyang, Hunan
Province, China
Raised in: Easton, CT USA
Currently resides in:
Chicago, IL USA
Age at adoption: 9 months

Dear Fellow Adoptee,

HERE IS ONE OF MY college essays that explains my feelings about my adoption and being Chinese. I know that my perspective is unique but I am hopeful that you might find it interesting, if not relatable. I am interested in your thoughts if you are ever inclined to respond.

—-

I was adopted as a nine-month old baby from Hunan Province by a Jewish father and a mother of Swedish- Anglo-Saxon ancestry, who'd spent her childhood growing up in Saudi Arabia. Navigating this already diverse mix of influences and cultures, my parents sought to reconnect me with my Chinese heritage, taking me to Chinese cultural events, keeping me in touch with other adopted children and, finally, bringing me to China, against my will, one summer. While they were admirably persistent, I continuously spurned their efforts, revealing an uncomfortable truth: I didn't feel Chinese. Not even a bit. Worst of all, the expectation to connect with other adoptees, based purely on the fact we came from the same country, not only led to a fair number of awkward social interactions but also profoundly puzzled, and later, offended me. We had all spent the vast majority of our lives in America: hadn't we proved ourselves, beyond a doubt, more American than Chinese?

What bothers me most is that, from the moment others lay eyes on me, they translate my Asian physical characteristics into a wealth of experiences and history that, in reality, I do not own. While most outsiders mean no harm, these assumptions feel deeply corrosive to 'my' efforts to carve out an identity, on my own terms. Instead of being asked how I 'choose' to identify myself, racially and ethnically, society categorizes me first into the simplest label as "different" (in America, this just means "nonwhite"), then brands me "Asian" and

"Chinese" in sequence, and stops there because the racial stereotypes seem sufficient. In contrast, because looking White is considered more ambiguous, my White peers are given a choice. Not only are they asked more frequently how they self-identify, this ambiguity allows them greater freedom in their answers, whether they choose to ethnically identify or not. Their identity is allowed to transcend both the color of their skin and their cultural associations. On the rare occasions when I, too, am asked about my origins, it is an appreciated opportunity for me to define myself past racial stereotypes.

Given the choice to identify, perhaps I would simply say I'm American. Considering there is no proven genetic basis for race, I could even call myself White. But that would just be bowing to yet another stereotype, and stereotypes are rarely, if ever, accurate. Identity is a richer construct than commonalities based on skin color, geography, religion, or ancestry. It is what we might 'choose' to take from these things but it can also extend far beyond, encompassing our experiences, our values, our preferences, our passions, our aspirations, our fears, our hopes, and our dreams. Fluid, inconstant, and ever-changing, identity is a product of our own volition.

In China, there's a funny name they give to people like me: a "banana" – someone who's perceived to be "yellow on the outside, white on the inside." I guess if you can boil identity down to color that would be an accurate statement. But clearly, a dichromatic label can't even begin to characterize my existence. And while no seventeen year-old I know would, or is expected to, claim they have a fully formed identity and I am no exception, there are some things I do know: I've been an opera enthusiast since I was five (yes, my parents took a five year old to the Met's 'La Traviata'); I count the ten minutes a day I take to read the old-fashioned newspaper as sacred; I've learned everything I know about perseverance from horseback riding; I fear loneliness but value independence; I am American; I pray to no god but have an inexplicable faith that those who meet me will understand that I am more than my ethnicity. I am certainly much more than a common fruit.

Sincerely,
May Silverstein

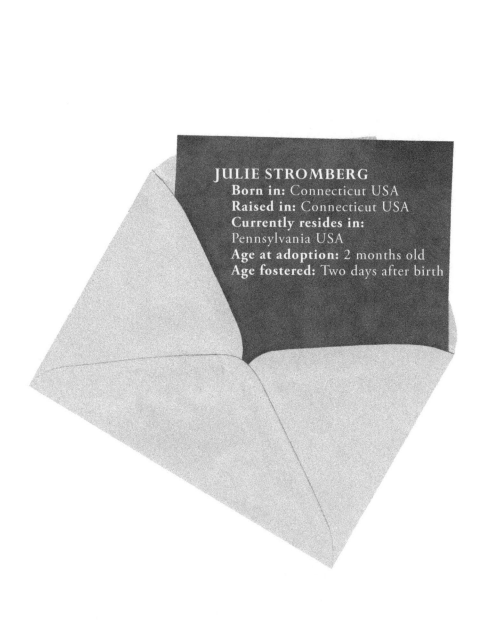

JULIE STROMBERG
   Born in: Connecticut USA
   Raised in: Connecticut USA
   Currently resides in:
   Pennsylvania USA
   Age at adoption: 2 months old
   Age fostered: Two days after birth

The Society of Adoptees and Fostered Persons

My adult adoptee pals, fostered adult friends, and I have often discussed how we wished there was some sort of secret handshake that we could share with our younger counterparts. Really, we have! Like, there you would be in the grocery store and one of us would walk by with an understanding look. Then we would quietly extend one of our arms with the hand shaped into a fist, and you would just know to give it a bump back. The truth is that we are all around each other and don't usually know it.

But imagine if we did...

Dear Wonderful You,

ONGRATULATIONS. WE, YOUR FELLOW ADOPTEES and fostered persons, welcome you into the Society of Adoptees and Fostered Persons (SAFP). As an adopted or fostered young person, you qualify for membership into this exclusive club where no non-adoptees or non-fostered-persons are allowed. Because we know that sometimes you just need to be around the people who truly understand you.

Yeah, we know. It's not like any of us actually signed up for this adopted and/or fostered life or anything. But we're here. We're in it. And we are the only ones who truly know what it feels like to be born of one family and raised by one or more other families. Which, to use young adult literary terminology, kinda makes us like our own Hogwarts School of Witchcraft and Wizardry house from *Harry Potter and the Sorcerer's Stone* or district from the *Hunger Games.* Or our own exclusive society like the SAFP.

Of course, the SAFP is not exactly a society that anybody intentionally seeks entry into. I mean, really. Ideally, we would have been born to our natural parents and raised by them. But we weren't and sometimes it seems like a lot of people don't want to hear that maybe we feel sad, hurt or angry about it. Fortunately, for members of the SAFP, it is more than okay to feel whatever it is that you feel about your own life experience. Within our exclusive membership, it is considered completely healthy and normal for an adoptee or fostered person to experience anger, sadness or confusion—and to express those feelings without being made to feel guilty or bad about it. This is because when you think about it, our experiences all started with the same thing. We were all separated from our original families. What happened to us from that point on might differ, but our emotions and thoughts on that initial separation are where we can find common ground and understanding.

That's the cool thing about the SAFP. Having our own exclusive society means that none of us are ever alone and that there is always someone around who understands you. Trust me. For every time that someone has told you how "lucky" you are to have been adopted or fostered, there is an adult adoptee or fostered adult member of the SAFP who has heard it too—recently. Yep, I am totally serious. We actually have non-adopted and non-fostered adults telling us how we should feel lucky to have been separated and removed from our original families. For some reason, they focus only on what they view as positive and dismiss what caused us to be adopted or fostered in the first place. Not to worry, the SAFP makes a point of recognizing that your life experience as an adopted or fostered youth is complicated and not something to be simplified, as some people often try to do.

Sometimes, these same people even try to inform us that we should be "grateful" for having been "saved" from whatever horrors would have been forced upon us had we stayed with our original families or in our countries of origin. Maybe you have heard similar statements as well. Or perhaps, this has been implied in other ways. Some of us adult adoptees and fostered adults have been told, for example, that our original mothers were not able to keep us but at least she didn't have an abortion. When people have said this to me, I have wondered why they expect me to be more grateful to be alive than someone who was not adopted. What's up with that? For some reason, these folks seem to not realize that we are quite capable of figuring out how we feel about our own lives. Perhaps some of us do not feel grateful or saved, which is perfectly normal and okay. As SAFP members, we do not tell each other what to think. We listen to each other instead—something that maybe these other people should try doing.

Fortunately, the SAFP Code states that no adoptee or fostered person should be made to feel any more lucky or grateful than anyone else for anything stemming from circumstances beyond our control. Additionally, the SAFP Code makes it quite clear that we are the only ones with the right to process and share our own stories. I bet you might know what I'm talking about here. Our adoptions and foster placements happen when we are minors and before we are legally recognized as individuals in our own right. Because of this, well-meaning, non-adopted and non-fostered adults sometimes speak for us and express thoughts on our behalf that might not actually represent how we feel as adoptees and fostered persons. Even as an adult adoptee, I have experienced one person telling another that "she was adopted and is totally fine with it" in reference to me. The truth is that I am not totally fine with everything pertaining to my adoption and I would prefer to be the one who shares my thoughts on the matter. When I am able to personally discuss my adoption experience, it helps me to remember that I am quite capable of speaking for myself. This is precisely why the SAFP considers the personal stories of adoptees and fostered persons to be theirs and theirs alone.

In honoring adoptees and fostered persons as unique individuals, the primary principle of the SAFP is affirming the inherent worth and value of all adoptees and fostered persons. It is our responsibility to remind each other of the tremendous dignity we all possess simply because we exist. As an adult adoptee and charter member of the SAFP, I am here to tell you that you are, in fact, an amazing person regardless of who created or raised you. You are not your adoption or foster placements. These experiences have shaped you, and perhaps provide the lens through which you view the world, but your worth is not defined by these circumstances.

As the newest member of the SAFP, know that we are here for you. You are not alone in this life experience. We care about what you think. Your feelings matter. We are listening. Because of you, the adult members of the SAFP are out here doing what we can to make things better for all adopted and fostered youth. You are our inspiration.

Yours truly,
Julie

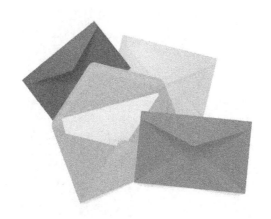

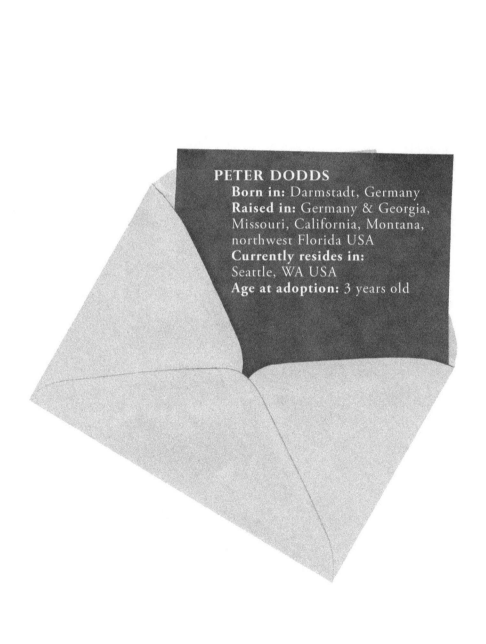

PETER DODDS
Born in: Darmstadt, Germany
Raised in: Germany & Georgia,
Missouri, California, Montana,
northwest Florida USA
Currently resides in:
Seattle, WA USA
Age at adoption: 3 years old

Dear You're Not Alone,

I HEARD YOU MIGHT HAVE BEEN bullied. Mocked, harassed and taunted because you're different. Maybe it was because you're adopted or in foster care. Maybe it's because you don't have the same color skin, are overweight or gay. I know how much it hurts because I was bullied as a kid simply for being adopted and being different. You don't have to face this on your own.

Bullying can happen to anyone and it is not your fault. There's nothing wrong with you. You shouldn't have been bullied and it's not oaky for others to do this. We are going to sort this out.

I was adopted from Germany into the United States. I always felt different, like I didn't belong and didn't fit in. Growing up in the U.S. wasn't safe. Americans thought Germany was evil. In schools teachers taught Germans were bad people. Kids used words like Hun, Nazi and Kraut to describe me and my people. I was forced to attend ceremonies where Americans celebrated defeating my homeland.

When I was in grade school I was playing a game of dodge-ball. The kid who was "it" stood with his back against a wall trying to dodge balls thrown by the rest of the group. Like everyone else, I wanted to be "it" and ran to the wall when my turn came.

Everyone else was fighting over how many balls they'd get to throw. Before the first ball was thrown, one boy yelled at me, "You're adopted."

"No I'm not," I yelled back.

"Yes you are. My parents told me you are. And you're a Nazi too." His teeth glistened like a ravished wolf.

"It's a lie. I'm not adopted," I shouted.

But the others joined in the taunting.

"Your real parents didn't want you."

"You're German. You're a Nazi."

The pack moved closer and started howling.

"Peter's adopted, Peter's a Nazi. Peter's adopted, Peter's a Nazi"

I broke through the mob and fled into a nearby forest. Why couldn't I just be like the rest of them? But I wasn't like them. Shamed, fright and pain seared my heart. I collapsed on a log, covered my hands over my face and sobbed.

The fear of being bullied made going to school or the playground a miserable experience. Being mocked and taunted made me feel lonely, unhappy and unsafe. I was always nervous it might happen again and dreaded being singled out for anything, even for something good.

So, I understand what you're going through and am on your side. I know how it feels but you are not alone. Here are a few things I've learned that might be helpful:

- You are not to blame and it's not your fault. The bully is to blame.
- Hang out with friends when a bully is nearby. There's safety in numbers.
- If you have someone you trust, talk about being bullied. Your parents, teacher, school counselor, a friend, or a sibling. Just talking about it can help make some of the hurt go away.

- There are lots of support groups for adoptees and foster care kids. Many of the people in these groups are likely to have had experiences like yours.
- If the bully physically hurt you or if they threatened to harm you, report it to a parent, teacher or an adult you trust.
- When I started playing basketball at school I made good friends and the bullies backed off. Maybe you could get involved in hobbies, sports or some kind of community activity. Having friends helps keep bullies away.

Years later I can look back on being bullied at the dodge ball game and realize that it made me a better and stronger person.

I'm strong, can overcome adversity and struggles in a healthy manner.

I have great empathy for people who are down trodden, especially for anyone that feels like they're different, a misfit, or not good enough.

Sometimes I try to help people and am surprised that it makes me feel good.

I wrote a book about being adopted from Germany and it includes the dodge-ball scene. I redirected all the emotional energy from being bullied and used it for something constructive. Now I'm working to have the book made into a movie and the dodge-ball bullying is one of the scenes.

One day you will know joy and happiness as powerful as the hurt, shame, fear and anger you're feeling from being bullied. Keep your chin up, take the next right step and great things will come your way!

Best wishes,
Peter

SOOJUNG JO
Born in: Seoul, South Korea
Raised in: Shepherdsville, KY
Currently resides in:
Southern California USA
Age at adoption: 3 years old

Dear Friends,

B E PROUD OF WHO YOU are. You might not realize it yet, but you have already accomplished so much: you have survived, and therefore everything is possible.

Losing one's mother is the most traumatic experience a child can have. This is not my opinion; it is scientifically, psychologically proven fact. The effects of your loss will reach throughout the rest of your life in ways both good and difficult, in ways small and large, in ways obscure and obvious. Every single effect is okay.

In response to the loss and subsequent effects, you might feel emotions across the entire spectrum: sadness, grief, joy, gratefulness, guilt, contentment, anger, loneliness, peace, and confusion just to start. All of those feelings are okay.

You might wonder why you were separated from your first mother, and it's possible (even likely) you'll never know. You might be told lies, or you might be told speculations, but someday you'll come to terms with the fact that you may never know. Separation is not the same as rejection. Perhaps your mother was too young, too poor, or somehow unable to care for you, and there was a part of her that desperately wanted to keep you. Or perhaps you were forcibly separated by another family member, or a legal but unscrupulous adoption industry that feeds demand, or illegal child trafficking. There is no justice in mother-child separation, and it hurts everyone involved. Your first mother has never forgotten you, not for a day or minute or second. A part of you will never forget her, even if you only knew her for a moment. You both share this bond of remembrance and longing. Not forgetting is okay.

You might never wonder why you were separated from your first mother, because you have a happy life and choose not to look back.

You might have completed your mourning, or repressed it, or not needed it because you had a wonderfully suitable mother-replacement to fulfill your early needs quickly. Not looking back is okay.

You might look different than everyone around you, and that may shape your experiences and development. You might experience racism or classism that your current family can't understand. You might be required to face certain challenges alone, with no one next to you who has walked that path before. In the struggle you will find a resilience that can't be taught. It's not an easy way to learn, but it's a good, noble way, and it's okay.

You might respond to the world differently than those around you. You might be more affectionate or less, more physical or less, more demanding or less, more connected or less, more loving or less. You are special because of what you have survived, and no one can judge or understand all the ways you are uniquely you. You will find your own way to be whole, and must not compare it to the so-called norms around you. Whatever ways you adapt to navigate your relationships in this complex world, they are okay.

You might change from one effect and response to another, flowing like water through a river. This might scare or confuse you – how can I feel so happy in one moment and sad in the next? You can because you are a beautiful, evolving person with an entire range of emotions and every single one is correct. No one can tell you that your feelings are wrong: you are the sky, and feelings are only weather. All the weather is okay.

You will go through all the stages of life – adolescence, young adulthood, parenthood, and beyond – and each might impact and develop you in a different way. Different aspects of your early loss will awaken in you at different times. Every phase of your evolution is okay.

You might reunite with your first mother and family. It might go well, like a storybook dream, or it might go terribly and send you back into the tailspin of loss. Remember that everyone is carrying their own burden, everyone has a story and struggle, and sometimes they will try to unload theirs onto you. Do not accept this unnecessarily. Sometimes you can only carry your own burden, and that's okay.

For every one of us who was ever separated from our first mothers, and therefore has survived the deepest, most profound trauma that any living creature can face, there are many correct ways to be. You're not alone in this experience, but you are exceptional in it. Be exactly the way you are, no matter how difficult. Challenge the world around you, or embrace it, with the sheer honesty of who you once were, who you are now, and who you someday will become. Shatter the myths of who you are supposed to be, annihilate the expectations of what a good foster child and adopted child are. Shock the world with your pure integrity and find your own way to become whole. There is no other way but yours.

Be proud of who you are. If you are faithful to the profundity of your loss and openhearted to your unique and evolving response to it, you will always find a way to be whole.

Sincerely,
Soojung Jo
Lost at age 2
Adopted at age 3
Reunited at age 36

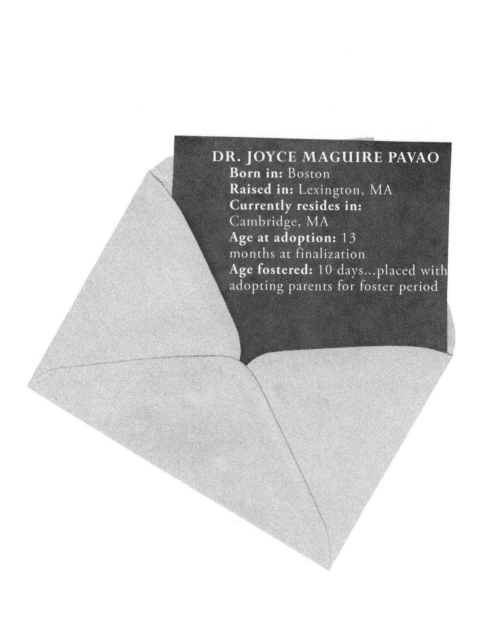

DR. JOYCE MAGUIRE PAVAO
Born in: Boston
Raised in: Lexington, MA
Currently resides in:
Cambridge, MA
Age at adoption: 13
months at finalization
Age fostered: 10 days...placed with
adopting parents for foster period

Thoughts of an Adoptee By-the-Sea

I HAVE SPENT AT LEAST A fraction of every summer of my life on Cape Cod. The most recent thirty summers in Truro. The nearest city to North Truro is Provincetown, which is an art community, a writers community, a place where Portuguese fishermen and gay and lesbian home owners and tourists and summer renters all reside happily together and watch out for each other.

It is said to be the very first landing place of the pilgrims before they went further inland to Plymouth. I have lived in several places in my life, but it was always clear to me that I could never live more than an hour from an ocean. Lakes are nice, ponds are peaceful, but an ocean is what I need nearby. Years ago I was asked to write about the seven core issues in adoption for a publication. When I was asked this time to write something about life as an older adopted person for teens to read, I thought... this would be the perfect piece to share with you.

I was born secretly. My birthmother told no one that she was pregnant, and she went to the hospital on a hot august day with 'appendicitis." I was the appendix. Her mother made quick arrangements to have me adopted out, and off I went to my adoptive parents. They were able to be my 'foster home' for the year that was necessary to wait for the finalized adoption. A year later, my name had changed, my life had changed, and my world had changed. My new world was fine. In some ways one might see it as 'better' than the one I had just left, and yet, in some ways it was sad because I was cut off from all that I held in my genes. It would take a book or two to tell the stories of 68 years of life. So I think it is easier to compact it into some Core Issues. So here goes:

Dear Adopted One,

I remember sitting with four of my best friends, who are all adopted as it turns out. This was about forty years ago, and we had the funniest hoot of a time just laughing and making fun of ourselves, and our adoptee neuroses. Last week I had dinner with two actor friends who are both adopted and, again, we had a lot to say about our place as adopted people.

I will share a bit about what we talked about. This is how we are allowed to joke about ourselves, but if you do it you're being 'birth-ist'. (I know for a fact that when one of our adoptive parent/ therapists run a group for adoptive parents and one of our birth mother/therapists runs a group for birth mothers, they have the very same kind of ways of making fun of certain aspects of their lives). This self-reflection and 'making fun of oneself' is important in terms of being self-aware – it's sort of like inner selfies.

It is quite true, we adopted ones were taken, and moved, and transplanted, and given new names and new identities as if we were in the FBI witness protection program!

Of course, we do have some trauma associated with our first loss, and with any other additional moves and losses. Wouldn't you? But the thing that comes along with the loss part is our very adaptive qualities.

We're adopted and we're adaptive!

We can get along anywhere as a result of this transplanting and replanting. Place us in a room with high society and royalty—we're fine. Our birth parents may have been kings and queens, in our fantasy after all. We're actors and actresses trying on many roles because we could be anyone, couldn't we? And we often don't even know who we are under the disguise. We could have been an entirely different person with an entirely different name and life! We started out as one person and then turned into another. Ta Daaa!! So we could be anyone.

We instantly know how to act and how to get along just fine, thank you.

Place us in a room with junkies and low-life thieves and we'll be hangin' out and talkin' trash with them in no time. Our birth parents could have been just like this! Place us in good schools and we'll either do just fine (aiming to please), or we'll be so busy trying to get the social thing down (we have to be accepted, after all) that we'll miss our assignments and do rather poorly academically. But we'll be working on something. We just adapt and adapt and adapt.

You all ('you' being society, the adoption system, and sometimes parents and professionals) made us think that our birth parents were poor and unable to parent, and so we gravitate toward a lower socio-economic group of friends at certain periods, or we work with this population in order to give something back to *our people*. We take what you say very seriously.

You don't even realize what you're telling us some of the time. If we're relating to what we think is our 'background' and you put it down in any way, it only adds to our losses in terms of our loss of self-esteem. So, please, love and respect our culture, love our race, love our religion and love our ethnicity of root family, as well as that which we gain from our family by adoption.

OK. Now back to talking about you... the young adopted.

Here are some core issues I referred to in the opening of my letter:

Intimacy?

It takes knowing who you are to know who you can be with another. So, we either get all dependent and mushy and enmeshed and then feel rejected, or we stay in our marginal stance. After all we are marginal people. We fit in two families (or more) while, at the same time, we fit in neither of these families completely. We are excellent bystanders, as we can see from any angle. (We make great therapists! We make great detectives! We make great friends and family members—although we can be hard to live with as we sort out our divided loyalty and loss issues.) We are eternally loyal, like a beagle. But if you hurt us too often you are dead to us. We know how to make people simply disappear...it is what happened to our birth family when we were put in a closed adoption.

Attachment?

We were uprooted. We attach really well over and over and over, but the roots are delicate after they've been torn and the tenacity wears down. We will reattach well only once, if the people we're

DR. JOYCE MAGUIRE PAVAO

placed with are also good at attaching (it takes to tango and to attach so it isn't all our job). But don't move us too often, or we'll have no ability to stick to it. Then we'll be better at moving from place to place to place, because that is what *society* will have taught us. We'll have a hard time with jobs and with career and with relationships. We learn very well and very early you know. It is *society* that teaches us all of this by taking us away and then placing us, and then taking us away and then placing us. It's their shortcoming, not ours that leads to attachment problems. We attach on the surface very quickly. It's part of how we adapt. We can't even walk into a hotel room for an overnight stay without rearranging some furniture and making the place comfortable so that we can settle. We need to bring along some transitional object— familiar objects— when we are in strange places. Our first familiar object (birth mother) disappeared!

Loss?

We can't find a thing! Loss is an issue that pervades. We deal with it in many different ways. We are pack rats and some of us keep everything —every shred of everything. We collect old things, 'useless' things, because this what society has often thought of us. We have to have one of every color of our favorite sweater...what if we lose one? People misdiagnose some of us as having ADD (Attention Deficit Disorder) but really, we all have this problem with distraction because it feels like...something is missing. Our rooms are cluttered and piled high with things that we can't lose, because we're trying to calm our feelings about the people that we've lost.

We misplace keys and things and joke about loss being a huge issue for us, because we are adopteds. Some of us go the other way and KEEP nothing. We give things away. We'd rather be in control and we'd rather know where things are, even if those things are with someone else. We live sparsely and can't bear to have anything that may end up being lost. It is the same issue, the manifestation is just different for some of us than others.

Anger?

I guess SO! How would you feel if people did things to you when you were asleep and unconscious and when you were an infant or small child? People destabilized your whole world and then, ta dah! You were a different person. It's okay. We can deal, but you bet there's going to be some anger. Not angry at the people (definitely our parents, birth and adoptive — they had their own problems and losses to contend with—we all did), but at the situation. We older adopteds, from the very closed era, can't stand secrecy and get very angry if people are clandestine or passive aggressive.

Just *TELL* us! Be frank! Tell us anything. Tell us the truth. The truth may hurt, but being kept from it is even more devastating. The truth is what we've always wanted. Openness and sincerity.

Is it so hard? Our anger is dynamic. It moves us to get involved politically. To want to change the world, because our world was changed so dramatically. This can be a good thing and often is! We can focus our anger and use it to challenge what is wrong and we can be agents of change, as we were infants and children of change. Change is our legacy and our strength as well as our downfall. We are changelings.

Humor?

Humor is the highest defense mechanism. We were quick and early to learn whatever we needed in order to survive. We are survivors. We learned it from our birth parents and we learned it from our adoptive parents. We can laugh at ourselves. We can laugh at the world around us and we can play. We have the gift of play and fantasy because we have lived in a world of fantasy and not-knowing for oh, so long.

Spirit?

We have an innate sense of spirit and spirituality. It doesn't matter what religion our birth parents had, or what religion our adoptive parents had. It is not about organized religion or disorganized religion. It is about something much deeper and more personal. It is about the archetypal themes in our lives by adoption.

It is about who we are, and where we come from, and where we are going. It is about why we are here, and what we will leave behind in the name of our fathers, and in the name of our mothers. Amen.

... Written with the help of the dunes, and the sea grass, and the ocean that surrounds me in Truro, on Cape Cod where I have spent many of my summers, some with my adoptive family, many with my family of choice, many with my child and extended family and many with my birth family. To adopteds, family is huge, and extends to the ends of the earth and if we adopteds are held properly as children, we hold many as adults.

We need to take care of the little adopteds of the world –you are magical.

Wishing that you have all of your truths,
Dr. Joyce Maguire Pavao

THOMAS PARK CLEMENT
Born in: Seoul, Korea
Raised in: Massachusetts
Currently resides in:
Indiana and Manhattan
Age at adoption: 6 or 7 years old

Dear Fellow Brothers and Sisters,

I WAS BORN IN THE MIDDLE of the Korean War and abandoned on the streets at age 4. I totally understand the reasons why I was abandoned because Korea did not accept mixed children born out of wedlock. My single Korean mother would have had a very difficult time surviving in such a harsh Confucianism society with me at her side. Poverty and social pressures are probably the two biggest contributing factors why you and I were relinquished. Fortunately, I was adopted from my orphanage when I was around 6 years old to a very loving progressive middle class family in America and grew up in Massachusetts.

Since I spoke no English when I stepped off the plane I thought I all of a sudden became stupid, really stupid. All those funny noises coming out of everyone's mouth were incomprehensible to me. Of course I was way behind in school because of this and my grades were terrible right up through second year of college. My favorite grade must have been 5th grade because I did it twice.

It's strange that although my new family loved and took care of me very well, I oddly felt isolated and alienated from them, not only them but from the whole community we lived in because I was the only Korean Adoptee. You may have these feelings too and it's only natural. It is difficult going through life feeling you are the only one and misunderstood with so many questions like, "Why was I orphaned?", "Who are my birth parents?" or "What is my real birthday?", "What is my real name?" You may have had the thought, "Hey, these aren't my real parents." "This isn't even my real country." So what is "real" anyway?

With existential questions like this floating around in your head it's no wonder that depression sets in from time to time. And just remember something a friend told me, "Suicide is a permanent solution to a temporary problem."

When I was a teenager, I had not a clue what I wanted to do later on in life. The best thing that took the sting out of my loneliness was having friends. You actually don't need a slew of friends; just one that you connect with will do and of course more will happen later on in life. I played guitar in a rock band and that was great for growing the tiny circle of friends I cultivated. Right up until I was 27 I was totally broke, only had a guitar to my name and the bank actually owned it.

I dropped out of college after two years because my grades really sucked, moved to Indiana and went back to college for a degree in Psychology, got married, had twin girls and to make a living I joined a carpentry crew building houses. This got old after a few years so went back to college and earned an Electrical Engineering degree from Purdue University. Getting a degree in college did wonders for my self-esteem because that was proof I wasn't half as stupid as I had always thought.

To make a long story short, I eventually became an inventor and started a medical device company named Mectra Laboratories. Currently have 37 U.S. patents and 4 pending. Just for the fun of it I also have a Publishing Company, Truepeny Publishing, an R&D think tank company, AcroVentions Laboratories, LLC and an export company, Elegro LLC.

I'm telling you this because when you are younger and your past bothers you, you have a lot of questions, doubts and fears at the present with no clue what your future will bring. Never give up. Be the master of your own destiny. Stay in school and study. Get a college degree. Have a family of your own. It's important that you don't dwell on the past and unanswerable questions. Perhaps in the future you may want to visit the country you came from or do a birth parent search. With DNA testing labs like 23andMe, locating blood relatives is fairly easy.

Guess I could go on and on. The most important thing I have to say to you is, take care of yourself. You are your worst enemy. Do things you like and connect with others. Get into sports if you can.

With social media there are 100's of adoptee/foster groups out there. You aren't alone. There are a quarter million Korean adoptees alone and I would venture to say many of them have had the same thoughts as you. My Facebook name is Thomas Park Clement. Look me up.

Sincerely...
Your older brother,
Thomas

SUZANNE GILBERT
Born in: New York City, USA
Raised in: Maine &
New Jersey, USA
Currently resides in: Greater
NY Metropolitan Area, USA
Age at adoption: 2 months old
Age fostered: first 2 months of life

Dear Wonderful You,

IF YOU'RE READING THIS NOW you are one of the leaders, the seekers. In my generation many people who went through foster care or adoption rarely asked questions because they were told the Courts had sealed their records. Why want to do something you can't, right? So they never searched for answers and convinced themselves they didn't have the right, or didn't have the curiosity. They went numb. Some have called it being in a fog.

I'm giving you advice I wish someone had given me, even though I don't know you. Crazy, right? So the first thing I need to admit is that you may already be handling things better, given you're reading this book, than someone else would. That applies to people who are in a situation that lets them give you advice right now. So before you read more, I want to honor the fact that you have lived and have lessons yourself to share!

Here are four pieces of advice I can share with you:

You're better looking than you realize!

I wanted to be an actress but people who look like me didn't get cast in movies or TV shows. A guy who directed laundry detergent commercials gave me the inside scoop: fair skin, blonde hair and blue eyes looked clean. I looked "ethnic". My adoptive mom bragged about how hard she looked to find dolls with brown eyes.

Boys asked me out in high school but I felt that the less I looked like my adoptive family, the soap commercials or even a baby doll, the less pretty I was.

Then one day I got pictures of my birth mother for the first time. She looked okay. In fact, she looked good. And I looked like her. That changed things and I started to believe the people who said I was pretty. There's something about seeing parts of yourself reflected in the features of blood relatives that makes you realize you look okay.

Call on your older self, love your younger self.

Back in Maine when I was a teenager I used to go sit on a particular granite ledge that sparkled under the setting sun and look out over the channel. There was a hypnotic splash to the waves rolling into shore. I would watch those waves and think about a situation on my mind that I wasn't independent enough to get away from yet.

I had a thought then that turned out to be useful, 'the adult who I will become in a few years will look back and get this'. Suddenly I had hope that I would live beyond this inescapable situation that couldn't last forever. Suddenly I forgave myself for not being able to handle it now; there was an older self, an adult me who would.

Promise to your self of today to be that adult. When you get to that age – five years from now or fifteen years from now – trust me, you will look back at the you of today with love.

You can even practice this by imagining yourself as a small, trusting but helpless baby. No matter what happened to you, you were cute and worthy of protection and love. Like all babies. Look back at that younger, helpless self with love.

Once you're older, not only will you be able to love your younger self, but also laugh at things that worried you or pained you today. You will be able to see the good. You'll be wise enough to see the beginnings of a resilient but kind person. You will see wonder-full you.

People you don't even know yet have love and hope for you; remember you are part of the human family tree.

Whether you are in a wonderful family or in a group home, as you grow older you will find a larger chain of people who care about you as a member of their tribe. Sometimes a tribe is a good extension of a family. It's better than isolation. We all need family, not just at your age, but at any age and being part of a tribe can provide that.

For me it's my faith, Judaism; for a friend of mine adopted from Korea it's the Korean church near her apartment. For many it's been communities of searchers and activists online and in person who become their extended family.

Now, older than you I define my "close family" as *some* of the relatives from my adoptive family, *some* from my birth families, and all of my in-laws. But when I was your age I couldn't picture being married, being a parent and step parent, being estranged from the sister I went through so much with, and I *knew* I would never meet my birth parents and siblings. I was wrong: you just don't know!

I have rich networks beyond family, tribes beyond these families. Your concept of family will expand, too, and you will meet more people on this human family tree.

Keep healing and exploring and integrating. You have real losses: people who haven't had these exact ones may dismiss them. They take for granted what they have. Once you find, you will enjoy your hard-won authenticity.

People may think what's done is done: your story is all told or you're not curious. I thought that at your age. You may not feel that it's legitimate for you to search. People may say don't bother.

But over two decades later I'm here writing this letter to wonderful you because there's a journey ahead of you.

Hope will launch you. Love will sustain you.

Don't let anyone make you doubt your right to take the journey. Having the name of a parent, or growing up in a nice new family, or a "bad" family of origin are not good reasons not to track down and solve the mysteries that are you. You have an adventure awaiting you.

Your story will be unique but there are many stories out there. Others who were touched by adoption, foster care or who lost birth stories due to surrogacy and infertility clinic practices have helped me identify over a hundred novels and short stories about a missing parent, identity and birth connections.

They are called search & reunion novels, genealogical mysteries, family identity dramas and quest novels. I posted as many links to them as I could find on a Facebook account called "Orphans, Adoptees & Birth Searcher Fiction" so you can find some, if you'd like. You have a story of your own to explore and tell. It can bring joy, pain and the peace of having tried to heal the past and find the truth.

So that's the advice I have to give you who are already wonder-full.

Praying for you,
Suzanne

J.S. LONDON
Born in: Taipei, Taiwan
to a Birthmother from
Jiangsu Province, China
Raised in: Laguna Beach,
California USA
Currently resides in: Southern
California USA, London & Spain
Age at adoption: 2 years old

Dear Wonderful You,

I DECIDED TO WRITE TO YOU and share a fictional story which is dear to my heart. Although fiction, it contains real names of my family members and the story itself has been passed through multiple generations of my family (including many adopted members).

The story is about a secret and sacred café, *Inspiration Ice Cream*, which has existed for centuries as one of the oldest and most venerable institutions of magic, but has never been listed in any phonebook or travel guide. My grandmother told me about this magical place, and just as she has passed it on to me, I would like to pass it on to *you*.

This secret rendezvous café has helped many people with their creative and spiritual problems, blocks, and life hurdles. The café specializes in lost and forgotten flavors of ice cream and chocolates that have healing powers, but also sells unique *bonbons* and mouth-watering edible potions for all sorts of life troubles. It is a place, dearly beloved and frequented by only those in the know, where you can also meet your life mentors (from the past, the present and even the future) to record your 'Inspiration Line' (a version of an Ancestral Line whereby those related to you are not necessarily blood kin but are spiritual kin), share delicious desserts, create and restore harmony, balance and Magic in your own life. Guard it well and its magic will nourish you.

Hope to meet you soon,
Jennifer

A ND SO, THE STORY BEGINS with a six year old girl, in 1917, exploring her old home's attic...

There were no lights. Only a small black door marked the attic entrance.

Lucy, age 6, sniffed and scrunched up her nose, while holding a candle in her right hand. Once inside, the room smelled moldy and musty. "You'd think we were in the 1800s, not in 1917 Los Angeles!" she announced loudly, as if to chase away the presence of ghosts. Cobwebs brushed against her face as she reached the farthest corner of the attic. *There it is!* She ran over to a large crate hidden behind boxes.

Lucy shook off the warning of her mother's voice inside her head—*You must never go up in the attic without me.* She sucked in a deep breath. Then she turned back and touched one side of the crate. She thought...*There must be something here.* As she rubbed off a thick coat of dust, she stared into a rough and stormy sea scene, carved into the wood. It looked like an old chest, much older than ones she had seen in the antique store with her Mama. She traced the delicately made images of waves and sailing ships with her fingertips, wondering what was inside. Then, suddenly, a mysterious wind came and blew out her candle.

Her two small eyes, adjusting to the dark, remained still. Her heart was beating fast. She waited a moment to allow the darkness to fade. She winced, and held her left palm across her heart while closing her eyes and drawing in a deep breath, as her Mama had shown her how to do whenever she felt nervous. When she slowly opened her eyes, at first she saw nothing.

Although the chest was closed, she could see a light slowly appearing inside. She blinked. The light was about the size of a pincushion. But then as it grew her mouth fell open. She watched with fascination as the light circled round and round inside the chest, shining through the wood.

"Oh my," Lucy stared, intrigued, as the light traveled and stretched from one end to the other, lighting up the entire chest. Suddenly, with the light she could see that the chest wasn't black or even brown, but a sort of green wood with beautiful pieces in red, green and purple jade. The light slowly grew stronger and stronger, and then lit up the keyhole. It was so radiant that she was blinded by the brightness. But as she slowly opened her eyes the top of the chest began to lift open, flooding the attic with sparkly light. Then Lucy saw the most amazing thing.

Inside the chest was a miniature city, dancing and filled with life. There were small children laughing and playing. And ice skaters and a singing carousel. There was even a tower. She looked at couples and friends chatting in cafés, spilling onto the streets with life and energy. And a feeling of love filled Lucy's heart. She watched boats steaming down a river under bridges, and then she watched the small light float down a series of ever-smaller streets, until it traveled down an alley. Once there, it seemed to blink at her. Then the light faded away. She held her breath.

Taking a small magnifying glass from her pocket, she carefully examined the alley and the little building where the light had disappeared inside. She read... "Inspiration Ice Cream."

Then she looked again. This time she moved the magnifying glass more slowly as she carefully read the words out loud:

- Inspiration Ice Cream Café & Tea Parlour -
Rive Gauche, Paris
BY INVITATION ONLY VIA LETTER REQUEST.
MAKE YOUR RESERVATION
FOR THE FUTURE YOU NOW.

Lucy gasped. *What does that mean?!* She sat back, deep in thought. When she leaned forward again to peer inside the chest, she accidentally brushed up against a jade piece on the side. *BOING!* Out popped a secret drawer from the bottom of the chest. And inside, a sign read: "POST BOX for the Inspiration Ice Cream Café, Paris, Rive Gauche, 75007." Lucy carefully lifted off the top of the box, and suddenly a stack of letters a foot high, glittering with gold edges, appeared. Lucy began to read the first letter:

Dear Mother,
I've been waiting my whole life for this moment. Do you think
Great Gran Lucy will recognize me? It's been such a long time

since I heard her voice. I don't think I will be able to greet her without crying. How embarrassing! But of all people, she is the one I know will understand. I wish that you could come with me, but I understand if it makes you nervous since I will be meeting my blood relative.

Great Gran Lucy thinks that I should type my letters to her, but how will she recognize it's me if they're typed? She must see my handwriting, so she can feel me, feel the spirit in my words, touch my letters with her elegant fingertips (does she paint her nails?). We'll only have a short while together, so I want to tell her as much as I can before we actually meet.

I've been dreaming about her my whole life. We're meeting at Inspiration Ice Cream, the Rive Gauche ice cream parlour for gourmands, nestled in the heart of the 7th arrondissement in Paris. Since I have lived across from Rue de Bac, I'll be able to show her my old haunts in the neighborhood. Do you think I will recognise her? Even though we have never met, I somehow know that I already love her. I somehow know that when I see her, smell her, touch her, I will be home. I wonder which flavour of ice cream will she order?

Love,
J.S.

She has the same name as me, thought Lucy as she scratched her head. *And I wonder who J.S. is?* Lucy then picked up the next letter...

Dear Great Gran Lucy,

I have never been to China. I hope this doesn't disappoint you. I hope that I don't disappoint you. I don't feel Chinese. In fact, I'm not really anything at all. I'm from southern California, but most people wouldn't think that by looking at me. I speak American English, French and Californian Spanglish, but I'm ethnically

Chinese. My greatest hope is that we can be great friends. It will be our one day at Inspiration Ice Cream. The day that I will always remember.

I learned that people need to book several years in advance to reserve a table. How did you know that we would want to meet there? You must have made the reservation when I was very small, maybe even when I was just born. When I become a Gran (if I ever become a Gran), I will do the same. I will make a reservation years in advance to meet my granddaughter at Inspiration Ice Cream. We'll make a plan to meet there by coincidence, as if it wasn't a plan at all. Inspiration Ice Cream is a place where dreams have already come true, after all, and the things that I've always wanted to share can—at last—be shared with you, beautiful great grandmother.

I will tell my grandchild that the most magical things in the world happen in ordinary places, small places like this special café that was (like me) almost never born. I will tell them about how we met and shared ice creams and views of the Eiffel Tower and walked along the Seine. I will tell them about your stories, your dreams. Inspiration Ice Cream will be a part of their history, theirs to share, too. It will be the place where we can all meet, even those of us who never meet, the place where we will all remember, especially those of us who cannot remember. Because sometimes you have to be the spark, the one who makes doors appear where once there were only great walls. When you're already gone, who can afford to wait any longer? I hope you don't mind, but I've written the rest of my letters by hand.

Looking forward to meeting you soon,
J.S.

Lucy slowly put the letter down. Her hand was trembling with excitement. *Could it be…could she be…?* She wondered. She had heard stories from her *Mama* and *Baba* about her own grandmother's travels abroad, where she had collected and exchanged many recipes that were passed down in the family.

"Lucy!" she heard her older brother's voice calling from downstairs. "Lucy, *Mama* says it's time for dinner!!"

Just as she was about to respond, a strong wind swept through the attic and knocked the top of the chest closed with a loud BANG! She jumped. Her heart pounded like a drum. Rain suddenly poured down and thunder and lightning flashed outside the attic window. Flustered, she was about to put the two letters back on top of the pile and close the bottom drawer when an even stronger gale suddenly threw the attic window open and a bolt of lightning in the shape of a jagged-Z lit up the sky.

"*Lucy Jing! Baba says you mustn't be late for dinner again!!*"

"I'm coming!" she shouted as the window shutters banged open and closed, sending the letters flying into the air like feathers, scattering in every which direction. "Oh no!" Lucy cried. Released from their box, the letters burst into flames in mid-air, burning together and creating a giant bright white light that thrust Lucy back against the attic wall, rattling the eaves and shaking the walls. She covered her face to shield herself from the brightness and the heat as the wind sent her hair flying towards the heavens. When Lucy blinked open her eyes, to her amazement a large bright golden door in the shape of a circle had appeared in the wall, and was slowly opening.

"*LUCY!*"

Lucy hesitated, glancing nervously towards the hallway. Then she looked back. On the other side of the golden door Lucy could hear voices and smell the most delicious aromas of warm chocolates, with hints of lavender, rose and mint. She reached out her hands, closed her eyes, and stepped through.

MEI-MEI AKWAI

ELLERMAN, PHD
  Born in: New York City, NY USA
  Raised in: Western Massachusetts
  & Vermont (USA), Denmark
  Mexico, France, Italy
  Currently resides in:
  Massachusetts & Vermont
  (USA), Italy
  Age at adoption: 7 months old
  Age fostered: from 10 days
  old to 7 months old

Dear Wonderful You,

WHAT A PRIVILEGE AND JOY it is to welcome you as a special member into our vast family and worldwide community! Born continents apart, in teeming cities, isolated rural areas, small towns or villages, each of us has a unique story. Yet a powerful common bond, an invisible, indestructible thread links us as sisters and brothers. Without uttering a single word, no matter what the differences in nationality, ethnicity, race, religion, culture, language, gender or sexual orientation, we instinctively "know," we "understand." We can identify with each other's intimate feelings, fears, and dreams, even the ones that we may keep secret, afraid that no one else can intuit their depth and complexity. So far apart, yet so close. And the book you are now reading will further strengthen our connection in unimaginable ways.

Despite what you may believe, none of us are alone. *You* are not alone. Embraced by ever widening circles of other adopted and fostered youth, many just a few years older than yourself, and by countless adult adoptees, you moved to the very center of our thoughts and outstretched arms the moment you picked up this volume of letters. *You now belong.* Just reach out in any way that comes naturally. One or more of us will immediately respond, listen to your story and be there for you.

I picture you holding *Dear Wonderful You,* your heart skipping a beat or two before peeking at the first pages. Your eyes are bright, your body tense, eager. I trust that the words we have offered and the heartfelt messages we have written exclusively for you will resonate and bring comfort, reassurance, even tears of recognition. If feasible, we would have sealed them in individual glass bottles or entrusted them to carrier pigeons to deliver to you in person. Realistically, a book is far more likely to reach you!

And now, as your older sister, I invite you to take a leap of faith. Join me on a brisk walk around a beautiful lake I circle from late fall through the cold New England winters and well into spring.

"Look around you!"

Towering trees surround us: pines, maples, oaks, and huge flowering shrubs, lilacs and rhododendrons. Let your gaze sweep across the vast expanse of the lake, with its innumerable inlets and hidden coves, teeming with life, both unseen beneath its surface and above. You will spot flocks of ducks with iridescent green heads as well as the gregarious Canada geese and majestic swans, both of which mate for life– a fact that always touches me.

"Let's pause for a moment. Listen to the sounds of the woods."

They rustle with scampering squirrels, echo with croaking frogs and the chirps and trills of songbirds. Whether under sunny skies, rain, fog, buffeted by snowstorms or caressed by soft spring breezes, they are a world unto themselves, magical, insulated from strife and human concerns– a place of peace.

Given that twilight is my favorite time, it is unlikely that we will encounter a single other person as we meander down the well-beaten dirt path, cushioned with pine needles.

"Be brave. Follow me. I will keep you safe."

Autumn is upon us. The leaves are turning. Many have already fallen like a gentle rain, creating a regal carpet of reds, oranges, yellows and variegated browns that all but obscure the underlying deep ruts and tangled protruding root systems. For me, this obstacle course is symbolic of the hurdles and stumbling blocks we encounter on our serpentine journey through life. We either learn to sidestep them or, preferably tackle them head-on and overcome them, even if repeated attempts are required.

As we pass by the open waters, families of ducks, the gangly adolescents not quite ready to strike out on their own, trail behind in their parents' wake. Several pairs of swans that return year after year prefer to congregate in private enclaves. The sociable geese swoop in and out, oblivious to the presence of the other birds.

"Feel the wind suddenly pick up."

A cloud of multicolored leaves swirls in a dizzying vortex, reminiscent of the emotional turmoil we experience at various points in our life, often when least expected.

The sight of the multi-hued whirlwind conjures up a deluge of powerful memories: the morning that three of our gigantic Great Pyrenees jumped upon me, tails wagging, and their rough tongues lathered me with kisses. I was two-and-a half and ended flat upon the ground in tears. The feeling of estrangement when my mother and I moved to Denmark for eight months when I was four. Dwarfed by colossal Nordic men and women, at first I spoke not a word of Danish and was unable to communicate though normally a garrulous child. Less than a year later, I found myself the center of attention in the colorful open markets of Mexico City and enrolled in an international kindergarten, the only Asian child. Recollections of a small school in Southern France float to the surface. I see myself, somewhat bewildered and lost, perched in a front row seat in a classroom that comprised five grades, all taught by the same teacher. And finally I retain vivid memories of my numerous years in the Italian school system, grappling with yet another language, culture and extremely rigorous curriculum. I attended a public elementary school for two years, a Catholic convent school for three, both in Alassio on the Ligurian coast, and subsequently slaved through five years at a top classical high school in Florence, before moving on to the University of Geneva. My mother encouraged, pushed and supported me throughout these numerous transitions. She taught me to believe in myself and was convinced that I had the strength to brave and surmount all challenges. Although there were some battles I faced strictly on my own, in the end she was right. We are far more resilient than we often realize.

Exposed to different countries, tongues and ways of being from age four on have taught me that there is no one place I consider home. During my adult years I have traveled the world, in search of knowledge of others and myself. Over the past decade and a half, I have visited and lived in China six times, in pursuit of my origins, both adoptive and biological. I have uncovered ancestral and existing family ties in China, Thailand, Korea, Denmark, France and beyond discovering more than I had ever imagined possible. The greatest gift is to feel that one belongs, and I, as a global citizen, feel at home no matter where I land. Perhaps it is because my destiny was to journey through space and time, weaving together the threads of my family history into a tapestry of multi-layered connections, from the distant past to the present...

Tension fills the air as all of nature prepares for the arrival of the blustering winter winds and bone-chilling cold that freezes leaves into curled up cocoons. Soon blizzards will blanket and transform the woods, pathway and lake into an indistinguishable sea of blinding white. The lake will gradually ice over, restricting open shallows to tiny pools. Left no choice, our winged friends, at times bickering to defend a small patch of water, finally surrender and huddle together. This past winter, one of the swans lost his partner. A solitary mournful figure, he silently glided back and forth, enshrouded in his cloak of grief.

At some level, these aquatic creatures remind me of us. Though they remain within the confines of their chosen lake, they are forced to continuously adapt to a changing environment. All of us, fostered and adopted, once safely cradled in our mother's womb, emerge into the world to find ourselves abruptly snatched away from the woman who nurtured us for nine long months, or was forced to surrender us. The reasons are innumerable and though they may plague us and appear unjustifiable, more often than not, our mothers had no other choice.

Unlike the aquatic birds, we do not have the luxury of swimming in the same waters. Instead, we are compelled to adapt to entirely new surroundings, frequently more than once: an orphanage filled with strange faces, a foster parents' home, and the household with our new family whose members most likely bear no resemblance to us. We either become skilled actors and appear to fit in seamlessly, barely causing a ripple, even though we feel like an outsider, or else we slip into the new configuration, sensing that we have landed in a safe haven, unconditionally accepted and accepting. Others among us may remain aloof, painfully disconnected, and unable to trust.

Learning to adapt to changing circumstances depends on fortitude, flexibility, unmitigated support, and the strength to develop a firm sense of identity and self-preservation.

"Identity..." Perhaps one of the largest issues we face as adopted and fostered individuals. It goes without saying that at some point in our life, whether when quite young or at an advanced age, we are going to wonder, "Where did I come from?" "Who was my mother?" "Why did she relinquish me?" To be severed from our original parent and native land, be it a foreign nation or simply another part of the country in which we now abide, creates a deep loss that everyone must acknowledge: ourselves, our [adoptive] family, and all those who love us. They must understand that there will always be questions, whether voiced or not, lingering doubts, and an aching, though perhaps deeply hidden "void." Loss, abandonment and rejection are the main triggers to which we remain vulnerable throughout our lives. These issues need not control our every thought, but deserve to be fully recognized and honored.

Some of us will search for our origins, fueled by enticing dreams. We may be successful. Some may discover that reality differs considerably from our fantasies. Some of us may never discover the truth about our roots. No matter what, we cannot go through life constantly looking backwards, allowing ourselves to be imprisoned by the past. While never forgetting that we have a past, an unknown past, we are best served by living in the present and looking forward to the future. One thought we can all hold on to is that somewhere on the planet there is a person who will never forget us, who will love us from afar, even if unknown and faceless except in our imagination. A mother never forgets. May this knowledge always comfort you. Most of you have families who have embraced you and made you theirs. You are fortunate to belong to at least two worlds, your adoptive family and, as of right now, your immense extended family of fellow adopted and fostered adults.

My mind keeps straying to the figure of the lone swan. When I was six, my parents divorced for well-founded reasons. My father, an intelligent, delightful, highly talented jazz musician and businessman, lost his way. From then on I grew up with my mother, the most loving and ferociously protective and loving person I have ever known. She prepared me for the countless trials and challenges I would encounter as a child and adolescent, equipping me with manifold skills to handle them.

My mother was a scintillating example of a survivor who at age eleven left China, her homeland, to be educated with her four siblings in the US. Though all the children had guardians and tutors, they only saw their father every five years when he was granted leave of absence [he was a Danish diplomat who lived in China]. They were separated from their Chinese mother in early childhood; then finally reunited with her as adults in the States for two fleeting years before she returned to her motherland. My mother and her siblings grew up to be extremely independent and comfortable in their own skins. They gave generously of themselves to others and advocated for any number of humanitarian causes. They provided wonderful models to emulate.

Mother and I led an exciting life. We spent short periods of time in the US, but as mentioned, otherwise lived in Denmark, Mexico, France and then in Italy for many years. The only places where I experienced bullying and taunting for being Asian were in schools in the US. Two episodes stand out in memory. When barely 7, I vividly recollect being forced to the center of a large circle while children chanted, "Chinky, chinky Chinaman, daughter of a laundry man…" It went on and on until I almost collapsed from dizziness. I felt increasingly hemmed in, unable to escape the whirling blur of faces and the words that sliced through me like piercing blades. The second time I was eight, a temporary pupil in an all-White school in Darien, Connecticut. There had been a snowstorm the night before, the first of the season. Everyone was flush with excitement, wearing a brand new snowsuit, boots and mittens. I was reluctant to join the others for recess due to previous incidents, but finally ventured out. Within seconds, I found myself pushed to the ground and being rolled in a mixture of mud and freshly fallen snow, kicked and spat upon. A teacher finally extricated me, my teeth almost biting through my tongue as I refused to cry. Mother arrived within minutes, upbraided the Principal and stormed out holding me safely in her arms.

Thanks to a severe case of chicken pox, I never returned to that school. For the first time Mother took the opportunity to explain in simple but explicit words the basis of racial prejudice and discrimination. She essentially attributed the children's intolerable attitudes and cruel behavior to ignorance and a gut or learned response to anyone who appeared to be "other," or "different." She emphasized that it had nothing to do with me and who I was. Their conduct reflected their parents' views and revealed lack of education coupled with unjustified feelings of superiority and privilege. Her all-encompassing love swiftly healed all superficial wounds but the fact that the memories still linger, speaks to the deep impact of what occurred. I wouldn't be surprised if many of us, especially the younger generation have had similar or far worse experiences.

In today's world in which social media can become an instrument of torture to those targeted, the issue of bullying is even more prevalent and pernicious. Just remember, what counts is who you are, how *you* perceive yourself and that you are fully aware of your innate value. Don't be swayed by opinions of others, by taunts or name-calling. You have every right to hold your head high, be profoundly proud of your heritage, whatever it may be. And now you have us to turn to for support and comfort. Never hesitate to reach out. *We are here for you.*

Returning to our walk, I wish that in the space of the next half hour I could magically lead you through the different seasons and transformations that will take place all around us. I will do my best by painting a series vignettes. In deep winter, the snow drifts pile many feet high, creating narrow tunnels through which one has to thread one's way. The path becomes treacherous, slick as a skating pond. Just before Christmas, a sudden burst of color mysteriously appears in a different spot each year: a secret Santa festoons a baby pine tree with garlands of cranberries and strings of popcorn for the birds; dazzling glass balls and delicate ornaments for passing onlookers. All tree tops are bedecked with white crowns, their branches partially clad in layers of powdery fluff or encased in ice. To survive the freezing temperatures the birds almost double in size as they produce extra protective plumage. Yet never do they appear as sleeker and more alluring than in winter.

This latter observation brings to mind an issue with which thousands of young people battle, especially throughout their teens and twenties, adopted and fostered youth in particular: outer appearance and body image. The desire to look thin in order to "appeal," to be "hot," to "be noticed," can lead to an obsession with one's weight, over-exercising and in severe cases to anorexia and bulimia. Or the opposite can occur. Those who lack self-confidence, who wish to become invisible, hide behind their bodies to avoid attracting attention. I wish to reiterate that the beauty and core values that count come from "within." Don't be swayed by TV ads, frighteningly skinny models and actors. You are beautiful *just as you are*. Accept yourself, believe in *You*, and love yourself. There is no greater gift than self-love. Of course we all have doubts, go through moments when we question our decisions and circumstances, but what ultimately matters is mustering the strength to overcome these hurdles, and benefiting from the lessons learned.

As the temperature begins to climb and the days grow longer, the ice, which has restricted all birds to tiny spaces above and hidden the fish and millions of other little creatures from our sight below, begins to thaw. Each day, new openings appear in the vast body of water. The weight of the winter snows on the bare tree limbs and heavily laden boughs of the evergreens, gradually lightens. One senses a lift in the air, the fragrance of approaching spring, and time of rebirth. Songbirds, ducks, geese and swans, even the deer leap into action and start to compete for food, space and nesting grounds.

Ah competition! That word, which so often translates, especially for adoptees, into an unacknowledged drive to be "perfect." We tend to set impossibly high personal standards, motivated by an innate compulsion to excel, not just in the eyes of others, but to prove our worthiness to ourselves. While I have always demanded the best of myself, competed against myself, and expected that my students live up to their potential, as well as my own children, I am acutely aware of the possibility of burnout and of even more serious consequences if one is unsuccessful. Pace yourselves, my young siblings. Let your curiosity fuel your imagination, hone your skills, stretch to your full ability, but also be gentle on yourselves. Don't feel that you have failed if you don't achieve the highest mark in your favorite subject; it is just one among thousands of grades you will receive over a lifetime. Whether you are drawn to dance, music, theater, art, sports or academics, just do your very best without placing undue pressure upon yourselves. The purpose of education is to learn to think creatively and critically and to freely explore the breathtaking richness of the intellectual and artistic worlds. You will shine no matter what. You already do!

And so you and I have come full circle, back to our point of departure. I am honored that you have followed me on our virtual and metaphorical journey around my favorite lake, and patiently listened as I shared my personal musings. I have sought to have you vicariously experience the seasons of the year, representative of the cycle of life itself. As a result, I hope that I have ignited in you an appreciation of nature as an invaluable, ever-present companion and source of solace. Even if you live far from a public park, a shimmering lake or shaded woods, you need only pluck a leaf from a maple or oak and examine it in detail to value the beauty and nurturing force of Mother Nature. Take a moment to gaze at the intricacies of a flower, encircle the sturdy trunk of a tree with your arms, feel the kiss of raindrops bathing your face, or raise your eyes to the heavens on a clear night.

Thank you for joining me. I somehow feel as if we've come to know each other quite well. In the brief time spent together, I have laid bare some of my vulnerabilities, and disclosed feelings and insights which have guided and sustained me on my own voyage. I hope that they will prove valuable as you embark upon the best years of your life: the many many decades that lie ahead.

Night is falling; a gentle hush has descended and a silvery mist envelops all visible and invisible surroundings. Far above, millions of stars beckon and vie for our attention while the half moon casts its glimmering light upon the limpid waters of the lake. Let's move forward a few feet, to the very edge of the shore.

"Look at our faces, reflected as clearly as in a mirror."

We are both smiling, warmed by our walk and a sense of greater closeness. After a few minutes I will slowly move back, but I want *you* to keep gazing at your glowing image that emanates self-confidence, power, the courage to remain true to who you are and the conviction that you will thrive. Rest assured, your newly acquired family will support and accompany you every step of the way.

With much love from Your Older Sister,
Mei-Mei

Contributor Biographies

JoAnne Bennett

After being placed for adoption at birth, Bennett's adoption journey has been winding and full of twists and turns, but she reflects on her many blessings — raising three wonderful daughters alongside her loving husband of 39 years. Her passions are writing and making a difference in young people's lives. Helping children see that they have voices that truly matter is her heart-felt desire. She believes that loving out loud and treating one another with kindness and respect is a way of positively changing the world. JoAnne's most recent credits include a contribution to the book, *Adoption Reunion in the Social Media Age, An Anthology,* a story in a book titled, *One for the Road* and a publication in *Chicken Soup for the Soul: Teens Talk Middle School.*

Email: tndrhrtjb@comcast.net
Website: http://storiesbyjb.com/
Facebook: https://www.facebook.com/Tenderheartjb
Twitter: @tenderheartjb

Thomas Park Clement

THOMAS PARK CLEMENT was born in Seoul, Korea in 1952.
He received a Psychology Degree from Indiana University (1978) and two Electrical Engineering Degrees from Purdue University (1985/1987).

Clement also attended the University of Delaware, Bonn University (Bonn, Germany) and Berkshire College (Pittsfield, Massachusetts).

Clement is the recipient of numerous awards including:

* AKA Inaugural Role Model Award July 25th, 1999

*Distinguished Alumnus Award, Purdue School of Engineering, 2000 (one given per year from a pool of all Alumni)

*Appointed by South Korean President KimDaeJung to 2002 Advisory Committee on Unification

*Supplier of the Year Award 2007 by Healthtrust Purchasing group

Clement's U.S. Medical Patents include: 37 awarded, 4 pending

He is currently President / CEO of Mectra Labs Inc. started in 1988, a manufacturer and distributor of laparoscopic surgical devices.

Additionally he is President/CEO of Truepeny Publishing Corp, Acroventions Laboratories LLC and Elegro Inc.

In 2012, Clement published his memoir *Dust of the Streets*.

Clement is involved in humanitarian missions to countries in need of food and medicine. He received the President's Call To Service Award 2014.

Email: mectralabs@mectralabs.com
Facebook: https://www.facebook.com/
Alien8it (Thomas Park Clement)

Brenda Cotter

BRENDA COTTER is a lawyer, an adoptee, and the parent of two beautiful and amazing daughters adopted from China. She is thrilled to participate in this project with her daughter Charlotte. Brenda was born in 1956, grew up in West Springfield, MA and currently lives in Newton, MA.

Email: b-cotter@comcast.net

Charlotte Cotter

CHARLOTTE COTTER was adopted at five months old from Zhenjiang city, Jiangsu Province China and grew up in the Boston area. She is one of the co-founders of China's Children International, a global support and networking organization that aims to empower Chinese adoptees all over the world by providing an inclusive community for all of us who share this common beginning. She is currently an undergraduate at Yale University where she plans to major in East Asian Studies with a focus on China. In her free time, she loves volunteering in the community, practicing her Chinese by watching Chinese films, and walking her two dogs. She would like to dedicate her submission to her mother, Brenda, who has always been a supportive and guiding force in her life.

Email: charlottelin.cotter@gmail.com
Website: www.chinaschildreninternational.org
Facebook: www.facebook.org/groups/chinaschildreninternational/
Twitter: @CCI_Adoptees

Laura Dennis

LAURA DENNIS was born and adopted in New Jersey and raised in Maryland. She earned a B.A. and M.F.A. in dance performance and choreography, but gave up aches and pains and bloody feet in 2004 to become a stylish, sales director for a biotech startup. Then with two children under the age of three, in 2010 she and her husband sought to simplify their lifestyle and escaped to his hometown, Belgrade. While the children learned Serbian in their cozy preschool, Laura recovered from sleep deprivation and wrote *Adopted Reality, A Memoir*, available on Amazon. She blogs at *Expat (Adoptee) Mommy* and *The Lost Daughters*.

Email: laura@adoptedrealitymemoir.com
Website: www.laura-dennis.com
Facebook: https://www.facebook.com/AdoptedReality
Twitter: @LauraDennisCA

Peter Dodds

PETER DODDS was born in Germany, to a German mother and father. Relinquished to an orphanage, he was adopted by American parents, one of 10,000 German children adopted by United States' citizens during the Cold War. Peter's memoir, *Outer Search Inner Journey*, is the first book written on international adoption by a foreign-born adoptee. An avid writer and passionate speaker, Peter's delivered keynote addresses in New Zealand and Canada while his writings have appeared in numerous publications and websites. A former Army Ranger, he's now working on adapting *Outer Search Inner* Journey to film.

Email: aphpub@hotmail.com
Website: www.peterfdodds.com
Facebook: https://www.facebook.com/peter.dodds.566

Mei-Mei Akwai Ellerman (co-editor)

Born in the US and adopted at 7 months, Mei-Mei Ellerman studied at Boston University, the University of Geneva, and the Liceo Michelangiolo in Florence. She holds a doctorate in Romance Languages and Literatures from Harvard. After 30 years of teaching Italian literature and film at Boston area institutions, she now focuses on research, writing, social activism and Reiki.

A Scholar at the Brandeis Women's Studies Research Center and founding director of Polaris Project [leading anti-human trafficking NGO], Mei-Mei is deeply committed to abolishing modern-day slavery. She also serves on the boards of Chinese Adoptee Links International and Global Generations, regularly contributing to the ChineseAdoptee.com blog. Co-founder of the AN-YA Project, her involvement in adoption issues includes fighting against fraudulent adoptions and for universal access by all adoptees to their personal records.

Mei-Mei is working on two memoirs based on years of worldwide research and travel: *Circles of Healing, Circles of Love: A Labyrinthine Journey in Search of Connections*, the 27-year-long search for her Chinese biological origins, and a cultural biography covering 160 years of her bi-racial adoptive family history, *In Pursuit of Images and Shadows: A Chinese Daughter Ventures into her Mother's Past.* Most recent publication: Dedication and chapter in *Perpetual Child: Adult Adoptee Anthology.*

Email: akmellerman@gmail.com
Website: http://www.anyadiary.com
Website: http://www.brandeis.edu/wsrc/scholars/profiles/
ellerman.html
Facebook: http://facebook.com/meimei2
Twitter: @mellerma

Ming Foxweldon (白宜民)

MING FOXWELDON was adopted from Kunming, Yunnan, China when she was three and a half years old. She left China and moved to Wisconsin, where she met her older sister, and younger brother (adopted from another country). After a few years, her family moved to New Hampshire, where she spent much of her childhood.

Foxweldon attended both public and private schools. After graduating high school she chose to study at the University of Vermont. Four years flew by, she graduated with a B.A. (Chinese Language (Mandarin) and also minored in Anthropology.

In 2011, Foxweldon chose to study abroad in China, (Kunming), for 6 months. Additionally her involvement with China's Children International, as member and new committee member, opened new doors. Two years later she returned for more adventures in China and its neighboring countries. As a Chinese adoptee, her interests in China have only grown from art to zoo life. Her hopes are to continue this important work, and share ideas to others so that they may be more informed.

Foxweldon anxiously waits for what the future holds. She thanks the past for teaching her how to be present and what she can do to be better for the future.

Email: mfoxweldon@gmail.com
Facebook: www.facebook.com/ming.foxweldom
Twitter: @mingaling44

Suzanne Gilbert

SUZANNE GILBERT was given this name before she was relinquished by her mother and placed in foster care. She has reclaimed it for her writing. She shares many of the hurdles of international adoptees because her first mother lives overseas. That mother found her with the first phone call occurring one afternoon when Suzanne's adoptive mother was visiting – launching a journey for all of them. Eventually SUZANNE GILBERT searched successfully for her birth father and siblings.

It was through search and reunion that she learned her ethnicity is Cherokee, Irish, Iroquois and Jewish. Today she is also an adoptive stepparent. One of the interesting twists in her blended family is that her adopted stepsons are part Iroquois, too. Her biological kids are the ones who strangers think are adopted because they are biracial (half Thai).

She worked as a journalist in Tokyo, Boston and New York, and spent part of her childhood on the coast of Maine. Her first novel *Tapioca Fire* is about an international adoptee and the crime her quest uncovers. It traverses the rich search & reunion subculture populated with sleuths, search angels and political activists.

Gilbert is working on a second novel that intertwines the stories of secret fathers.

Email: intermarketdirections@gmail.com
Website: amazon.com/author/suzannegilbert
Facebook: https://www.facebook.com/suzanne.gilbert.39
Facebook: www.facebook.com/AdoptionSurrogacyBooks
Novel: http://www.amazon.com/Tapioca-Fire-Suzanne-Gilbert/
dp/1495305759/

Rosita Gonzalez

Adopted in 1968 at the age of one, Rosita is a transracial, Korean-American, Holt International adoptee. Her road has been speckled with Puerto Rican and Appalachian relatives, including her perfectly-blended, multiracial sister, the natural child of her adoptive parents.

While quite content with her role as a "Tennerican," her curiosity has grown recently as her children explore their own ethnic identities. She has discovered that her children, the second generation of adoptees, have inherited her racial ambivalence. As a result, Rosita has recently started her search for her natural family. With the help of G.O.A.'L., she visited Korea in August 2014 and fell in love with her birth country. When she is not supporting her children on their individual paths, Rosita spends her time as an art educator, ceramicist, art photographer and activist. She is passionate about issues of race, gender and adoption. She shares her adventures as an adoptee and parent on her blog, *mothermade*.

Email: mothermade.design@gmail.com
Website: http://mothermade.blogspot.com
Facebook: mothermade, the blog
Twitter: @mothermade
Instagram & Pinterest: mothermade
Other: The lost Daughters website (www. lostdaughters.com) as the Feminist Columnist

Lynn Grubb

LYNN GRUBB was placed into closed domestic adoption as an infant and adopted through the Cradle of Evanston, Ilinois. She grew up with her adopted brother and parents in warm and cheerful Centerville, Ohio. She graduated from Wright State University and has worked in the legal field for the majority of her career, including volunteering as a child advocate for her local Juvenile Court, CASA/GAL program. Lynn has been married to Mark (her biggest supporter) for 23 years, has a 20 year old son named Matthew and became an adoptive parent to a beautiful daughter in 2005.

After finding her maternal birth family in 2006, Lynn became a contributing author to an all-adoptee writing project, Lost Daughters. Since that time, she has contributed to several anthologies, including *Perpetual Child: Dismantling the Stereotype* , *Adoption Reunion in the Social Media Age*, *The Lost Daughters: Writing Adoption from a Place of Empowerment and Peace* and *Called Home: Lost Children of the Indian Adoption Projects.*

Lynn is passionate about adoptee rights and genetic genealogy, having taken three genetic DNA tests and blogging about her results at her personal blog: *No Apologies for Being Me.* Lynn is still searching for the paternal side of her family.

Email: lynngrubb104@gmail.com
Website: www.noapologiesforbeingme.blogspot.com
Twitter: @grubb_lynn
Website: www.lostdaughters.com

Lee Herrick

LEE HERRICK is the author of *This Many Miles from Desire* and *Gardening Secrets of the Dead.* His poems and essays appear widely, in literary anthologies and college textbooks such as *Indivisible: Poems of Social Justice* and *Visions Across the Americas.* He was born in Daejeon, South Korea and adopted at ten months old to California in the United States. He is a professor, poet, and parent. He lives with his wife and daughter in Fresno, California, where he teaches at Fresno City College and in the MFA Program at Sierra Nevada College.

Email: leeherrick@hotmail.com
Website: leeherrick.com
Facebook: facebook.com/leeherrick

Soojung Jo

SOOJUNG JO is a contributing writer for the *Lost Daughters* blog (www.thelostdaughters.com) and contributing author for several adoption-related anthologies in development. She wrote for the now-retired blogs *Faiths and Illusions* and *Grown in My Heart.* Soojung's connection to adoption is threefold: adoptee, biological mother, and adoptive mother. She was reunited with her first family in 2013, and is now learning to navigate post-reunion life with both Korean and American families. A memoir about her adoption and reunion experiences is in development.

Soojung lives in Southern California with her husband and four children, who supply constant inspiration and entertainment.

Email: soojungjo3@gmail.com
Website: www.soojungjo.com
Facebook: Soojung Jo

Lucy Chau Lai-Tuen

LUCY CHAU LAI-TUEN made in Hong Kong and exported to the UK as a transracial adoptee. Lucy is a dyslexic actor, published writer, filmmaker, trainer and transracial adoptee advocate, who loves Dim sum, Yorkshire puddings and tea.

First professional job, female lead in the British feature film *PING PONG* (1987), directed by Po Ch'ih Leong. First UK feature to look at the history and issues of the British-Chinese community.

Other films include *Secrets & Lies, Something Good: The Mercury Factor*

Theatre credits include: *Julius Caesar*-Bristol Old Vic; *Drink the Mercury* nominated for a TMA (first British East Asian actress to be nominated for a major theatre award); *Hungry Ghosts* Tim Luscombe. **Plenty** dir. by Thea Sharrock

TV credits include: *Prime Suspect 2; Eastenders; Lovejoy*

Radio credits include: *Words On A Night Breeze, Bound Feet and Western Dress.*

Lai-Tuen is currently editing her independent documentary *Abandoned, Adopted, Here*

2011 Lai-Tuen wrote & performed her solo theatre piece *There Are Two Perfectly Good Me's: One dead, the other unborn*, a play looking at the issues of growing up as a transracial adoptee. Lucy is hoping to tour internationally so is looking for a producer.

Lai-Tuen is working on two new full-length theatre plays.

Email: lucylaituenchausheen@gmail.com
Website: http://www.lucysheen.com
Facebook: https://www.facebook.com/ActorLucySheen
Twitter: @LucySheen & @ActorWriterTRA
YouTube - https://www.youtube.com/user/LucySheen

Jeff Leinaweaver, PhD

DR. JEFF LEINAWEAVER is an internationally-known storyteller, and sustainability practitioner who works with leaders, organizations and communities on how to use story and storytelling to create change and influence the emergence of a more globally sustainable and socially just civil society. Through the power of story and the study of narrative, Jeff is a leading voice on how storytelling creates our social worlds and sculpts our identities.

As a performing storyteller, Jeff shares in the telling of the old stories – myths, folk tales and fairy tales from many different cultures around the world. Jeff believes the old stories are alive and inform us on how to deepen our connection with each other, nature and our own mythic journey.

Additionally, Jeff represents a first generation of internationally adopted scholars and social researchers studying and re-framing the conversation on international adoption, global citizenship and human development.

Jeff holds a PhD in Human Development and Organizational Systems with a specialization in narrative systems and communication. His most recent publications on adoption include *Storytelling Narrative Marginality – on Becoming a Global Human*, and *The Coordinated Management of a Culturally Diffused Identity: Internationally Adopted People and the Narrative Burden of Self.*

Email: Contact through website: www.jeffleinaweaver.com
Website: www.jeffleinaweaver.com
Twitter: @globalzen

J.S. London

Writing as J.S. London, Jennifer *Bao Yu* 'Precious Jade' Jue-Steuck of Laguna Beach (Orange County), California, is a graduate of New York University's *Tisch School of the Arts* and Harvard University, where she was a Bill & Melinda Gates Scholar.

Born to a birthmother from Jiangsu Province, China, Jennifer was adopted by an American couple from Los Angeles in 1979.

She is founder of *Chinese Adoptee Links (CAL) International - G2*, the first global group created by and for the 150,000 Chinese adoptees in 26 countries, and is a co-founder of their *One World Blog* (ChineseAdoptee.com). Inspired by her (adoptive) mother's life and battle with ovarian cancer, *INSPIRATION ICE CREAM* is a foodie memoir fundraiser to raise awareness about the effects of adoption motherloss and child bereavement.

Email: jenniferjuesteuck@post.harvard.edu
Website: InspirationIceCream.com
Website: ChineseAdoptee.com

Dan Matthews

DAN MATTHEWS is a Korean adoptee currently living in Los Angeles and working in the entertainment industry. He was raised in the small town of Camarillo, an hour north of LA, with his parents Lynne, Paul, and Jamie (also adopted). He's currently working as a producer for International Secret Agents, an Asian American entertainment and production company owned by Wong Fu Productions and Far East Movement.

Email: akadandocu@gmail.com
Website: http://dan-aka-dan.com/
YouTube: https://www.youtube.com/user/DANakaDANtv
Twitter: @DANakaDAN
Tumblr: http://danakadan.tumblr.com/

Dr. Joyce Maguire Pavao

JOYCE MAGUIRE PAVAO, Ed.D., LCSW, LMFT, was the Founder and CEO of Center For Family Connections, Inc. (CFFC 1995-2012) in Cambridge and New York, Founder and Director of Riverside After Adoption Consulting and Training (AACT) 2012 to present, and PACT (pre/post adoption consulting and training) 1982 to present.

Dr. Pavao has done extensive training, both nationally and

internationally. She is a Lecturer in Psychiatry at Harvard Medical School, and has consulted to various public and private child welfare agencies, adoption agencies, schools, and community groups, as well as probate and family court judges, lawyers, and clergy. Additionally, she has worked closely with individuals, and families created by adoption, foster care and other complex blended family constructions.

She has developed models for treatment and for training using her systemic, intergenerational, and developmental framework The Normative Crises in the Development of the Adoptive Family and her book The Family of Adoption (Beacon Press) has received high acclaim.

Dr. Pavao has received many awards and honors, including the Children's Bureau/U.S. Department of Health and Human Services Adoption Excellence Award for Family Contribution (2003) and the Congressional Coalition on Adoption award for Angels in Adoption (2000).

Email: kinnect@gmail.com
Website: www.pavaoconsulting.com
Website: PACT (pre/post adoption consulting and training)

Kaye Pearse

KAYE was adopted, twice, both times in open, inter-family placements. Although all her parents are deceased, she was in reunion with her bio-mother for more than a decade prior to her death, and remains in reunion with her bio-siblings. After sampling a variety of career paths, from theatre & film to commercial insurance, Kaye finally found her calling in education. She currently teaches at the Middle and High School level, and spends time volunteering with various educational programs and numerous animal rescue groups. Kaye lives on a small farm where she spends her spare time gardening, beekeeping and tending to her cats, dogs, chickens and goats.

Email: AdultAdopteeKaye@gmail.com
Website: adoption-interrupted.blogspot.com

Karen Pickell

KAREN PICKELL is a columnist and editor at *Lost Daughters*, a communal blog written by and for adopted women. She grew up in a closed adoption, but reunited with both of her birth parents as an adult. She is married to an adoptive father of two children from a previous marriage; together they have two biological children and one rambunctious dog. Karen has published adoption-related poems, essays, and stories, including those in *Perpetual Child: Dismantling the Stereotype* and *Lost Daughters: Writing Adoption from a Place of Empowerment and Peace,* which she also co-edited. She holds a Master of Arts in Professional Writing with a concentration in Creative Writing. She aims by the end of 2014 to finish drafting the memoir that has been stalking her for the past several years. Besides reading and writing, she loves being in and near water, taking photographs, and making up harmonies to her favorite songs.

Email: adopteekaren@gmail.com
Website: karenpickell.com
Facebook: www.facebook.com/karen.pickell.writer
Twitter: @Karen_Pickell

Jasmine Renee

JASMINE RENEE has been writing music on guitar and singing for over eight years. She is studying secondary education with an ESL endorsement and a minor in Spanish at the University of Northern Colorado. She hopes to travel the world teaching English. She is involved in a sorority, Alpha Sigma Alpha and the CUMBRES program as well, which is a scholarship program for teachers that give students the opportunity to receive an ESL endorsement on top of their major. She is very excited to be a part of the *Dear Wonderful You, Letters to Adopted & Fostered Youth* anthology.

Email: jrpyne@msn.com
Website: https://www.youtube.com/user/JazzyReneeMusic
Facebook: https://www.facebook.com/jrpyne?ref_type=bookmark
Twitter: https://twitter.com/jasminerpyne
Blog: www.chineseadoptee.com

Matthew Salesses

MATTHEW SALESSSES was adopted from Korea at age two. His most recent books are an essay collection, *Different Racisms: On Stereotypes, the Individual, and Asian American Masculinity,* and a novel, *I'm Not Saying, I'm Just Saying.* He has written for *The New York Times, NPR, Salon,* the Center for Asian American Media, *Hyphen,* and most often for *The Good Men Project,* where he is a columnist and Fiction Editor.

Email: m.salesses@gmail.com
Website: matthewsalesses.com
Facebook: facebook.com/matthew.salesses
Twitter: @salesses

Liz Semons

ELIZABETH SEMONS is a freelance writer who just finished her memoir *Strength of the Broken*. Her memoir chronicles her life journey as an adoptee left to face the world alone. Elizabeth dreams of her story becoming a screenplay for television or film. She is currently working on a suspense screenplay called *The Lies Beneath Bliss.*

When Elizabeth is not writing she is working at the District Attorney's office. She is a Legal Assistant and has worked for Family Support for ten years. Elizabeth likes that she is helping families, but the real reward comes from helping children.

Elizabeth is also a songwriter and aspires to become professional. She has used her songwriting abilities to escape from her reality since childhood. It is through song she expresses her pain, emotions and thoughts. She uses songwriting as a form of therapy but she also has a lot of fun creating the lyrics, melodies and stories.

Elizabeth raised two children on her own. For many years she worked two jobs to make ends meet. Now that her children are grown, Elizabeth recently resigned from her second job to spend her time doing what she loves—writing. The creative world is Elizabeth's passion.

Email: Blessedliz10@gmail.com
Facebook: liz.semons.9@facebook.com
Twitter: @semonse1

May Silverstein

MAY SILVERSTEIN was born in Yiyang, Hunan Province, China and adopted when she was nine months old into a loving and supportive family. She attended the Hopkins School in New Haven, Connecticut, and is currently a freshman at the University of Chicago.

Email: maycsilverstein@gmail.com
Facebook: https://www.facebook.com/may.silverstein

Joe Soll, LCSW

JOE SOLL 조 살, the author of *Adoption Healing... a path to recovery* 1 for adoptees, 1 for mothers of adoption loss and 2 for both, co-author of *Evil Exchange*, *Fatal Flight* and *Perilous Passage*, is a reunited adoptee, psychotherapist and lecturer internationally recognized as an expert in adoption related issues. He is director and co-founder of *Adoption Healing*, an international, non-profit organization consisting of over 470 adoption agencies, mental health institutions and adoption search and support groups in 8 countries, representing over 500,000 individuals whose lives have been affected by adoption. Adoption Healing is dedicated to educating the public about adoption issues and reforming current adoption practices.

Mr. Soll has appeared on Radio and Television over 300 times, given over 150 lectures on adoption related issues and has been acknowledged, quoted or featured in over four dozen newspapers, books and magazines.

He has been portrayed as a therapist in a NBC Made-For-TV movie about adoption, played himself in the HBO Special "Reno Finds Her Mom", was featured in the 2000 Global Japan award winning documentary, "Adoption Therapist: Joe Soll" and in the MediaStorm 2011 documentary *Broken Lines* as well as profiled in the *International Museum of Women*.

Email: joesoll@adoptionhealing.com
Website: www.AdoptionHealing.com
Facebook: https://www.facebook.com/joe.soll
Other: http://joesoll.com/Mystery/

Julie Stromberg

JULIE STROMBERG is a reunited adult adoptee who spent six weeks in foster care before being adopted as an infant. She loves zombie apocalypse shows, fancy food, and her hard copy of Roget's thesaurus. A graduate of Loyola University Maryland, she holds a bachelor's degree in journalism and currently works as a marketing writer and digital content strategist for a large investment firm. Fortunately, she has other writing projects going on to offset all of the boring financial stuff at the office.

Email: julie@juliegmstromberg.com
Website: www.juliegmstromberg.com
Facebook: https://www.facebook.com/juliegmstromberg
Twitter: @JulieStromberg

Amanda H.L. Transue Woolston, LSW

AMANDA H.L. TRANSUE WOOLSTON is an author, speaker, and licensed social worker with a Bachelor's degree and a Master's degree in social work. Amanda has served the adoption and foster care communities through individual and family clinical work, group work, writing and presenting, and working for positive policy change. Her writing and presentations have reached broad audiences through multiple books, magazines, major news and radio interviews, and conferences, and she has engaged with legislators at the state and congressional levels on adoption policy. Amanda is probably best known for her personal blog, *The Declassified Adoptee*.

Email: Amanda@amandawoolston.com
Website: www.amandawoolston.com
Facebook: https://www.facebook.com/declassifiedadoptee
Twitter: @AmandaTDA

Angela Tucker

ANGELA TUCKER is a trans-racial adoptee, adopted from foster care – born in the South and raised in the Pacific Northwest. At the age of 25 she reunited with some of her birth relatives, and is still actively searching for another birth sister as is chronicled in the documentary, *Closure*. Angela holds a B.A. in Psychology, regularly gives keynote speeches at functions around the nation and is a contributing author for two adoption anthologies; *Woven Together* and *Perpetual Child: Adult Adoptee Anthology; Dismantling the Stereotype.* Angela's most recognized article is a piece entitled "Do Transracial Adoptees Know Anything About Transracial Adoption?" which fueled a twitter-storm and the ensuing hashtag #NPRgate. She also writes a column on Adoptees and ableism for *The Lost Daughters* and has been featured in *Psychology Today, Adoptive Families Magazine, Slate.com, and Huffington Post.*

Email: angela@theadoptedlife.com
Website: www.theadoptedlife.com
Facebook: www.facebook.com/closuredocumentary
Twitter: @angieadoptee

Diane René Christian (co-editor)

DIANE RENÉ CHRISTIAN founded the *AN-YA Project* in 2012, after publishing her debut novel, *An-Ya and Her Diary*.

As the founder of the *AN-YA Project*, Christian has edited/published *An-Ya and her Diary: Reader & Parent Guide* as well as Co-edited/published *Perpetual Child: Adult Adoptee Anthology, Dismantling the Stereotype.*

In 2014, Mei-Mei Akwai Ellerman joined Christian as the Co-founder of the *AN-YA Project*. Together they continue to work towards *"Lifting the literary voices of adoptees".*

Dear Wonderful You, Letters to Adopted & Fostered Youth is the third book Christian has edited and published under the *AN-YA Project* umbrella.

Email: DianeChristian@live.com
Website: www.AnyaDiary.com
Website: amazon.com/author/dianechristian
Facebook: facebook.com/AnYaProject
Twitter: @DianeRChristian

CPSIA information can be obtained
at www.ICGtesting.com
Printed in the USA
LVHW111500010519
616204LV00001BA/62/P